Rick Peters

JOINTERS AND PLANERS

HOW TO CHOOSE, USE AND MAINTAIN THEM

Sterling Publishing Co., Inc.
New York

Acknowledgements

Butterick Media Production Staff

Design: Triad Design Group, Ltd.
Photography: Christopher J. Vendetta
Illustrations: Triad Design Group, Ltd.
Page Layout: David Joinnides
Copy Editor: Barbara McIntosh Webb

Indexer: Nan Badgett
Proofreader: Nicole Pressly
Project Director: David Joinnides
President: Art Joinnides

Special thanks to the following companies for providing product and technical support: Bob Skummer and John Otto at Jet Equipment and Tools, Doug Stephenson of Makita USA, Inc., Jim Brewer and Karen Powers of Freud, Inc., and Torgny Jansson of Tormek. Thanks to the production staff at Butterick Media for their continuing support. And finally, a heartfelt thanks to my constant inspiration: Cheryl, Lynne, Will, and Beth.   **R. P.**

Every effort has been made to ensure that all the information in this book is accurate. However, due to differing conditions, tools, and individual skill, the publisher cannot be responsible for any injuries, losses, or other damages which may result from the use of information in this book.

The written instructions, photographs, illustrations, and projects in this volume are intended for the personal use of the reader and may be reproduced for that purpose only. Any other use, especially commercial use, is forbidden under law without the written permission of the copyright holders.

Published by Sterling Publishing Company, Inc.
387 Park Avenue South, New York, N.Y. 10016
©2001, Butterick Company, Inc., Rick Peters
Distributed in Canada by Sterling Publishing, c/o
Canadian Manda Group, One Atlantic Avenue,
Suite 105, Toronto, Ontario, Canada M6K 3E7
Distributed in Great Britain and Europe by
Cassell PLC, Wellington House, 125 Strand,
London WC2R 0BB, England
Distributed in Australia by Capricorn Link
(Australia) Pty. Ltd., P.O. Box 6651, Baulkham
Hills, Business Centre, NSW 2153, Australia

Library of Congress Cataloging-in-Publication Data Available

Sterling ISBN 0-8069-6755-2

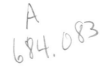

B
THE BUTTERICK® PUBLISHING COMPANY
161 Avenue of the Americas
New York, N.Y. 10013

INTRODUCTION

When I first started woodworking twenty-some-odd years ago, I was baffled as to why many of the projects I built just didn't turn out like I had hoped. Quite often there were gaps in glue joints and between parts that were joined together. It couldn't be the wood, I figured, since I had bought it from a reputable dealer and it was already surfaced on all four sides. I just assumed that it was nice and square and flat. With this in mind, I did what many beginning woodworkers do: I bought bigger clamps, thinking I could force the wood into submission. Big mistake.

The problem was that it *was* the wood. There wasn't anything wrong with it—it wasn't defective. It was just wood, and wood moves. It constantly reacts to changes in humidity and will continue to move well after it has been dried and surfaced. Boy, I sure wish that somebody had told me this when I started. The thing is, no matter where you buy your wood, and regardless of its quality, it's not going to be perfectly flat and square. The only way it gets there is if you make it so. And the two tools you'll need for this are the jointer and the planer.

The jointer will produce a true, flat edge that is the foundation of square stock. With the same machine you can then create perfectly perpendicular edges. The planer comes next to create absolutely parallel faces. The end result—square stock that when used for your projects will make everything go together easier and stay together longer.

In Chapter 1, I'll show you what to look for when choosing a jointer or a planer. I'll start by describing how a jointer works and then describe the two main types: bench-top and stationary jointers. Then I'll go over the different features of jointers and what to look for. There's also a flowchart to help with your decision making. Next, I'll jump into the planer, beginning with how it works and going over the two main types: bench-top and stationary. This is followed by information on the different planer features and what to look for. Here again, I've included a flowchart to help you choose the best planer for you.

Chapter 2 is all about jointer and planer accessories: everything from push blocks, stands, and knives to outfeed rollers and sharpening jigs. Chapter 3 jumps into basic technique for both machines. Each section begins with how to set up the machine, and then on to technique. For jointers there are details on edge-jointing, face-jointing, special cuts (like jointing end grain), and tips on how to work with short or long stock and how to remove cup. Then on to basic planer techniques, including how to square up stock. There's also information on using portable power planers.

Advanced techniques is the topic of Chapter 4. Jointer techniques include rabbeting, tapering a post, cutting chamfers and bevels, and even making raised panels. Planer techniques include tapering, working with thin stock, and creating molding with a planer/molder.

In Chapter 5 there are step-by-step directions on how to make a number of nifty jigs and fixtures for your jointer or planer. For the jointer there's a dust port, push block, and stand; for the planer there's a dust port and a nifty stand with flip-up extensions. And for use with either machine there's a mobile parts cart and an adjustable support stand.

Chapter 6 is rather beefy—there's a lot to cover about repair and maintenance of jointers and planers. For jointers, there's detailed instructions on cleaning and inspection, aligning the tables, lubrication, and three different ways to adjust the knives, along with information on how you can

sharpen them yourself. Then on to cleaning and inspecting the planer, lubrication, adjusting the knives, adjusting the cutterhead and outfeed rollers, and replacing brushes. Finally, I cover in detail how to replace motors and how to repair and maintain a portable power planer.

In Chapter 7, I'll describe problems that you'll commonly encounter on the planer and jointer, along with their solutions. Problems with jointers include rough cuts, chip-out, uneven cuts, ribbed and rippled cuts, and burning. Also what to do when the motor bogs down and how to avoid snipe and reduce excess vibration. Problems with planers include the ever-present snipe, ribbed cuts, rough cuts, chip-out, and motors that bog down.

All in all, this makes for a comprehensive guide that will help you choose, use, and maintain a jointer and a planer. Armed with this information, I hope that you'll use these tools with greater confidence to handle a wide variety of jobs around the home and shop.

Rick Peters
Spring 2001

1 CHOOSING A JOINTER OR PLANER

Square stock. It's the foundation of successful woodworking. It doesn't matter how sharp your tools are or how precise your jigs are—if the stock isn't square to begin with, the project likely won't turn out right. And no matter where you buy your wood—it won't be square. Period. The only way it gets square is if you make it so. And the two tools you'll use to do this are the jointer and the planer. These two tools, along with the table saw, make up the triangle of tools that form the foundation of any woodworking shop.

It's sad that many beginning woodworkers blame themselves for poor-fitting joinery and failed glue joints, when it's often caused by using off-the-shelf lumber, purchased at a lumberyard or home center, that's "surfaced four sides" (S4S). This stuff just isn't square.

Wood is an organic material that is constantly moving to react to the changes in its environment. "Air-dried" lumber sitting outside in a lumberyard isn't dry. When you bring it into your shop, it will start losing moisture and move at the same time. After it has had a chance to acclimatize (say, three weeks), then you can begin to work with it by squaring it up.

In this chapter, I'll start by describing how a jointer works (*opposite page*), so that you'll be able to better judge the different types and models out there. Then I'll go over the two main types of jointers—bench-top and stationary—and describe the differences between them, including their advantages and disadvantages (*pages 8–9*).

Next, I'll help you wade through the many features to check for when looking to purchase a jointer, everything from bed width and length to infeed/outfeed tables and ease of changing blades (*pages 10–13*). To help make the decision even easier, I've included a flowchart that will point you in the right direction (*page 14*).

Then it's on to planers, starting with a generic description of how they work (*page 15*) and a look at the two main types, bench-top and stationary (*pages 16–17*). This is followed by a close look at the features you'll find, with an emphasis on cutting capacities and motor size (*pages 18–19*).

For those of you with space limitations, I've included a section on combination machines like a jointer/planer and a planer/molder (*page 20*). Finally, there's a flowchart to help make your planer purchase easier (*page 21*).

HOW A JOINTER WORKS

Every jointer consists of two parallel tables with a spinning cutterhead in the middle that shaves off small amounts of wood from a workpiece that's passed over it (*see the drawing below*). The stock is fed into the cutterhead by way of the infeed table, and the outfeed table supports the freshly jointed workpiece both during and after the cut.

The knives of the cutterhead (anywhere from two to four) and the outfeed table are set to the same height. The infeed table on all jointers slides up and down to control the depth of cut when the height-adjustment wheel or knob is rotated.

On some larger jointers, you may find an adjustable outfeed table as well. The big advantage to this

is that you can sharpen the knives in place, and the outfeed table can then be adjusted to match their new height.

A fence runs perpendicular to the infeed and outfeed tables to support the workpiece so that the adjacent edges end up a true 90 degrees. On most jointers this fence is adjustable to allow for bevel cuts.

BASIC JOINTING ACTION

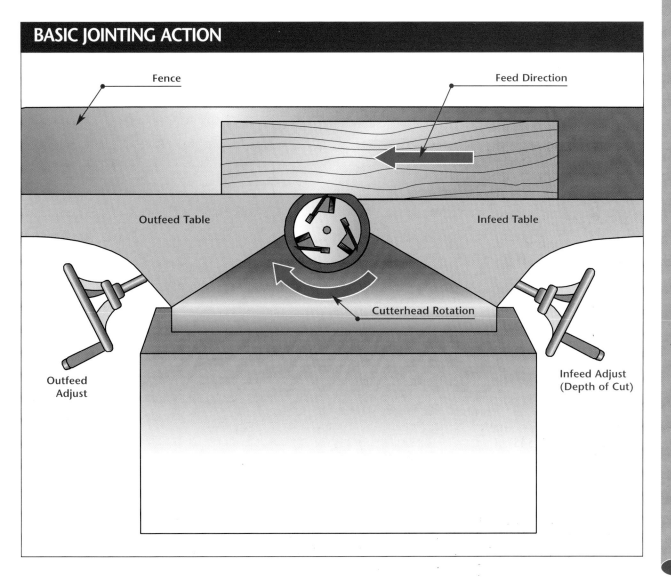

Fence

Feed Direction

Outfeed Table

Infeed Table

Cutterhead Rotation

Outfeed Adjust

Infeed Adjust (Depth of Cut)

BENCH-TOP JOINTERS

Bench-top jointers like the one *shown here* have limited use in the woodworking shop, primarily because of their short bed and underpowered motor. They do, however, work fine for short stock on limited runs. I know a number of woodcrafters who find this type of jointer more than adequate for their needs—this is especially true for those folks where space in the shop is limited. The diminutive size of a bench-top jointer makes it easier to shoehorn it into a small space.

For woodworkers who are building furniture, however, the short bed length is a real problem—it's difficult to accurately joint long boards, even with some form of additional support (such as an outfeed roller; *see page 28*). Although these small jointers often have a reasonably wide bed (6"), you'll be hard-pressed to get a smooth cut when face-jointing stock that wide. For one thing, the universal motor just doesn't have the power to handle the job. If you do try to make this cut, the already loud motor will literally scream trying to handle the load. The only advantage to a universal motor is that it's easy to vary the speed—most small jointers have a speed adjustment that will allow you to better match the planing speed to the material.

The other advantage of a bench-top jointer is its price: Most sell for well under $300.

ANATOMY OF A BENCH-TOP JOINTER

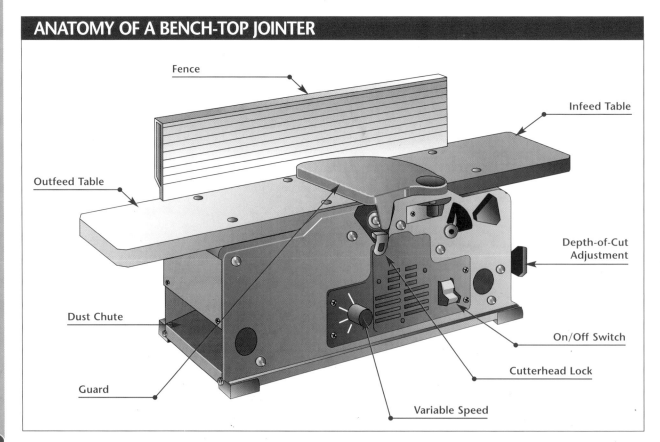

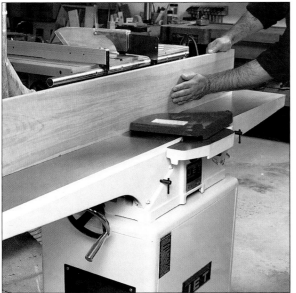

STATIONARY JOINTERS

from 6" up to a whopping 16". Many woodworkers find that a 6" jointer will do the job; but if funds and space permit, an 8" jointer is a better choice.

As the jointer bed widens, the tables lengthen. And the longer the tables, the more accurate and easy it is to straighten and flatten lumber. Smaller 6" jointers are typically driven by a ¾- to 1-hp induction motor, while the larger 8" models typically have a 1½- to 2-hp motor. Stationary jointers are available with open or closed stands. I always prefer a closed stand, since it's a whole lot easier to control dust and chips. Most models come with a dust port so that you can hook it up to a dust collector or shop vacuum. Prices range from $400 to $1,200 for 6" jointers and $600 to $2,300 for the larger units.

In addition to having wider, longer tables and beefier motors, most 8" jointers have a larger-diameter cutterhead that holds more knives. The larger the cutterhead, the more it cuts nearly parallel to the grain—and the smoother the cut. More knives at a higher RPM also means a smoother cut.

A stationary or floor-model jointer is a better choice for the average woodworker because the length of the bed is better matched to the width of the table (*see the drawing below*). Stationary jointers range in size

ANATOMY OF A STATIONARY JOINTER

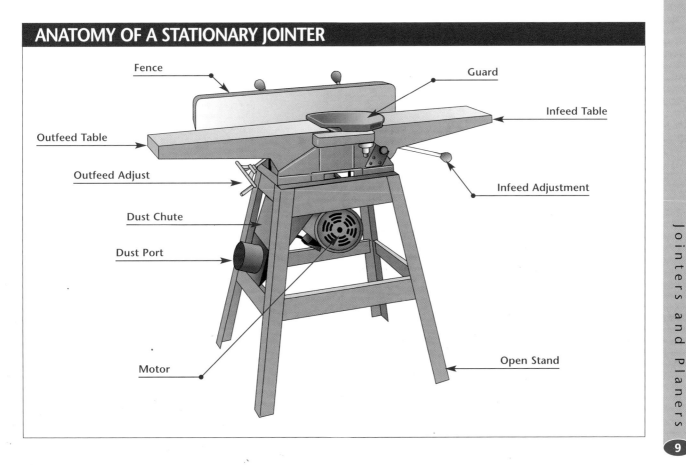

Fence

Guard

Infeed Table

Outfeed Table

Outfeed Adjust

Infeed Adjustment

Dust Chute

Dust Port

Motor

Open Stand

Bed Width The width of a jointer's bed determines the maximum cut. Although the two jointers *shown here* have similar bed lengths, the jointer *on the right* has a much wider bed: 8⅜" versus 6". Most woodworkers opt for a 6" jointer because of cost, but end up wishing they'd purchased an 8" jointer. The extra 2" makes a big difference when preparing rough stock—you'll often encounter boards that are wider than 6". With a 6" jointer, you'll need to rip the board before you can surface it.

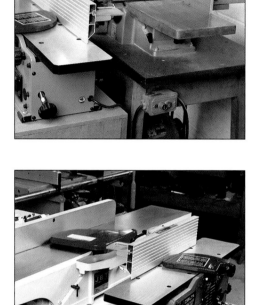

Bed Length As I mentioned previously, the longer the bed, the easier it is to flatten and straighten lumber. With short beds (*like the jointer at right in the photo*), it's all too easy to end up with a bowed board because the ends of the board aren't in constant contact with the bed. The long bed on the jointer *at left in the photo* fully supports the stock, creating an accurate reference to make a truly straight cut. If space is a problem, you can try supporting the workpiece with outfeed rollers (*see page 28*), but they won't do as good a job as a long bed.

Motor Size and Type The two types of motors you'll find on jointers are universal and induction. Bench-top jointers utilize universal motors and can tackle only small jobs. Stationary jointers feature a heavy-duty induction motor designed for heavier loads. They spin the cutterhead via a belt (*see the photo at right*). Obviously, the higher the horsepower and current rating, the stronger the motor. Note that most 8" and larger jointers require 220 volts to run. This is another reason many woodworkers end up with the smaller 6" jointers—they run off 110v.

Guard One of the most often overlooked features of a jointer is its guard. Look for one that has a strong return mechanism to guarantee that the knives are never exposed when jointing. Also, make sure that the guard is removable: There are some techniques where it will get in the way—rabbeting (*see page 47*), making raised panels (*see page 51*), and face-jointing wide stock. The guard should also be adjustable in height and must cover the knives regardless of the position of the fence—move the fence to both extremes to ensure that it does.

Infeed/Outfeed Adjustment Since the infeed adjustment is the main adjustment for a jointer, it's important that the adjustment mechanism be both easy to use and accessible. My preference is for a hand wheel (*like the one shown in the photo*), but some woodworkers prefer the lever style common on some models. Regardless of the handle or lever, make sure that there's a positive locking mechanism that will prevent the table from shifting out of position during use. Whenever possible, select a jointer where both the infeed and the outfeed tables are adjustable.

Knife Changing To be honest, changing knives on a jointer is a hassle. That's why it's important to check out any jointer you're interested in to see what the procedure is for changing knives. One feature that's nice is a cutterhead lock; see the red metal bracket that flips up to lock the cutterhead in place *in the photo at left.* This prevents the cutterhead from rotating out of position as you adjust the knives. Also look to see whether the gibs (the metal bars that clamp the knives in place on the cutterhead) are secured with bolts or screws. I've found that Allen-head screws are often easier to adjust than bolts.

Stand Although you probably wouldn't think that the stand for a jointer would have much of an impact on overall performance, it does. A stand that is both heavy and well constructed will help considerably to dampen vibration that can lead to a rippled or inaccurate cut. When looking for a stand, choose one that's made of heavy-gauge metal and that's bolted together. Add lock washers, if they're not supplied, when you bolt the stand together to prevent the nuts from working loose over time. For the optimum in dust control, select a closed base—it's a lot easier to capture and remove dust and chips.

Single versus Variable Speed Jointers with induction motors generally have one speed, determined by the RPM of the motor, the pulleys, and the diameter of the cutterhead. The manufacturer of the jointer designed the system for best performance, so it's important always to replace pulleys and belts with identical parts. Universal motors (*like the one shown here*) often feature variable speeds that allow you to match the cutterhead speed to the material.

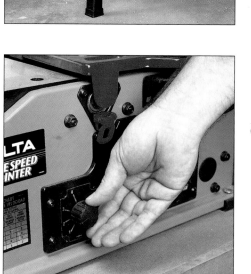

Dust Ports Jointers create a surprisingly large amount of dust and chips. Regardless of the stand chosen, it's important for your long-term respiratory health to capture as much of this debris as possible. Most closed stands are easily adapted for dust control by covering the chip chute with an adapter like the one *shown in the photo at right.* It is possible to capture dust and chips on an open stand—it just takes a bit more work (*see pages 59–61 for more on this*).

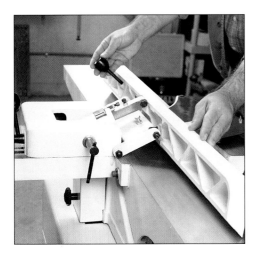

Fence The fence on a jointer is one half of the critical equation that creates perpendicular adjacent edges. The fence on a quality jointer should be easy to adjust back and forth across the bed, as well as having a positive locking mechanism. It should also feature linkages that allow you to tilt it when making angled cuts. Looks for built-in adjustable stops that set the fence at 90 and 45 degrees. Here again, make sure the locking system is positive and easy to use.

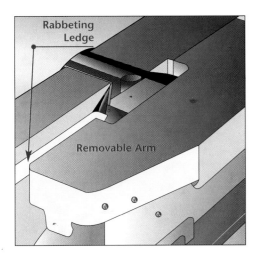

Rabbeting
Ledge

Removable Arm

Rabbeting Ledge Another feature to look for in a jointer is a rabbeting ledge, like the one *shown in the drawing at left*. A rabbeting ledge is a notch milled into the side of the outfeed table that allows the unrabbeted portion of the workpiece to clear the table. Rabbeting on the jointer is a terrific way to produce clean, crisp rabbets—as long as the rabbet runs *with* the grain. For more on rabbeting, *see page 47*.

PORTABLE POWER PLANERS

A portable power planer is one of those tools that fall between categories. Technically, it's neither a planer nor a jointer. Although the name implies that a power planer is a planer, it isn't. It's not capable of thicknessing stock so that the opposite faces end up parallel. A power planer acts more like a jointer, except that you move the tool over the workpiece instead of the other way around. Since the "bed" of a power planer is so short, it can't straighten or flatten boards like a jointer. What a power planer really is is a motorized hand plane. It's a terrific tool for removing a precise shaving from a project. Trim carpenters love these because they can remove a lot of material in a short time. Power planers make quick work of trimming a door to fit, chamfering an edge, or beveling a part. But beware, care must be taken to control these small but powerful tools. I prefer to limit their use to rough work and then switch to a hand plane or scraper for the final finish cuts.

CHOOSING A JOINTER

Choosing a jointer is a fairly simple process. Start by identifying the type of work that you do. If you work primarily with short stock and won't be working the machine very hard, a bench-top jointer will do the job. For the more serious woodworker who is working with longer and wider stock, you'll want to purchase a stationary jointer—either a 6" or an 8" model. If you've got the room in the shop, I heartily recommend buying an 8" jointer if you can afford it. I realize they're quite a bit more expensive, but I can't tell you how many woodworkers I know who purchased a 6" jointer and then realized they should have bought the larger 8" version. I also recommend buying or making a closed base for your jointer. Enclosing the base is the easiest way to capture and convey dust and chips away to a dust collector. Enclosed bases also keep the motor, bearings, and belt cleaner—so they'll run smoother and longer.

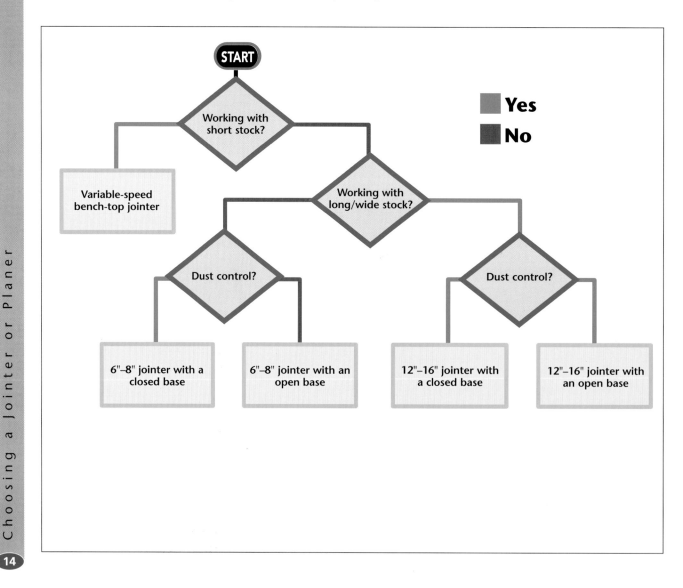

Regardless of how different planers are manufactured, they all work similarly. A workpiece placed on the bed of the machine is fed in until the infeed roller grips it (*see the drawing below*). The infeed roller may be rubber or metal with serrated edges (*as shown here*) to afford a better grip.

The infeed roller presses the stock firmly against the bed and pushes it forward into the revolving cutterhead, which holds two to four knives.

On heavy-duty planers, there's a metal bar called a chip breaker in front of the cutterhead that breaks off chips lifted by the cutterhead and helps direct them out of the planer.

Larger planers also often employ a pressure bar after the cutter-head to hold the stock firmly against the bed and prevent it from lifting up after the cut. The outfeed roller (usually rubber or nylon) grips the stock and pulls and pushes it out of the planer. Some planers incorporate metal rollers into the bed, set at a slightly higher level, to help reduce friction.

BASIC PLANING ACTION

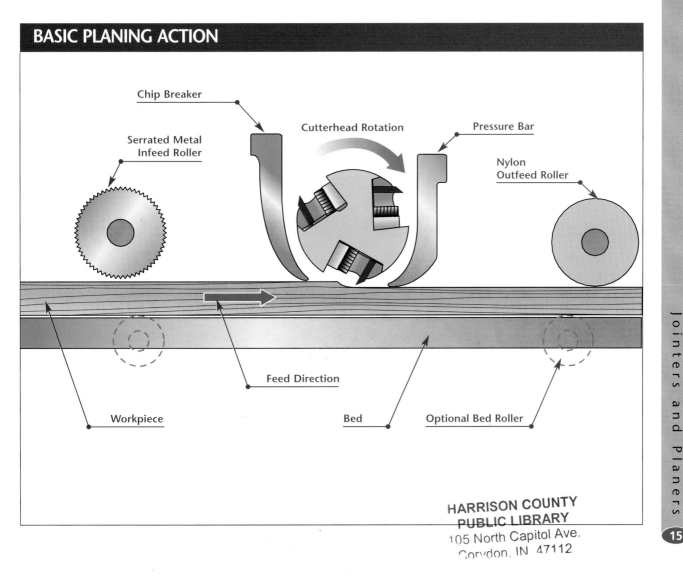

Chip Breaker

Serrated Metal Infeed Roller

Cutterhead Rotation

Pressure Bar

Nylon Outfeed Roller

Feed Direction

Workpiece

Bed

Optional Bed Roller

Jointers and Planers

BENCH-TOP PLANERS

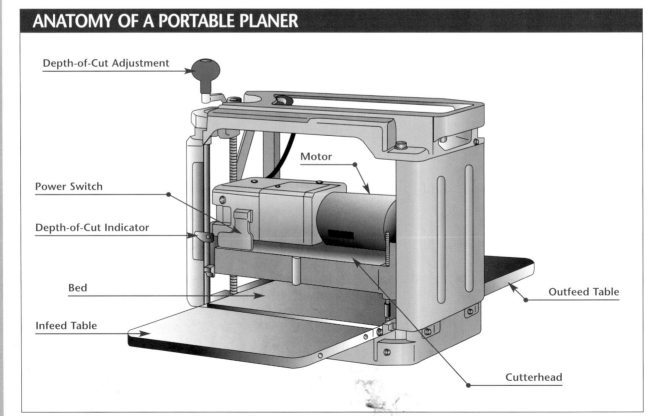

Up until about 1985, most home woodworkers could only dream about owning a planer. Until then, planers were giant beasts weighing upwards of half a ton and costing thousands of dollars. Most required 220 volts to operate and were found only in professional shops. But that changed with the introduction of the AP-10 planer by Ryobi. Diminutive in size (about as large as a suitcase), the AP-10 used a universal motor to make it highly portable—and at a price of around $400, it put this essential workhorse within reach of most hobbyists.

Since then virtually every tool manufacturer has introduced their own version, and you can often find them for under $300—most can thickness-plane stock up to 6" thick and 12" in width. Although bench-top planers do a decent job of leaving a smooth finish, they do have some drawbacks. Unlike their heavy-duty cousins (*opposite page*), bench-top planers don't use serrated metal infeed rollers. Instead they use rubber rollers—the disadvantage to this is that they don't afford as good a grip on rough lumber, and often skip or stall when dressing rough-sawn stock. They also don't incorporate a chip breaker or pressure bar, so the finish can suffer and snipe is often present (*see page 121 for more on this*). But as these tools continue to evolve, many manufacturers strive to improve finish, reduce snipe, and add features such as depth stops, accurate depth indicators, and other features that make a portable planer a solid investment.

ANATOMY OF A PORTABLE PLANER

Depth-of-Cut Adjustment

Motor

Power Switch

Depth-of-Cut Indicator

Bed

Outfeed Table

Infeed Table

Cutterhead

STATIONARY PLANERS

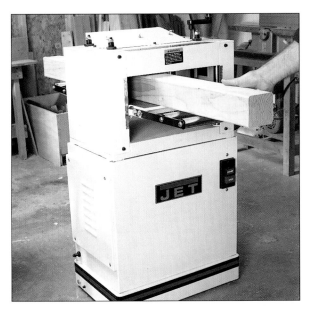

It's easy to understand why many woodworkers get confused when trying to decide between a portable planer and a stationary planer. One reason for this is that many small stationary planers have cutting capabilities similar to a portable planer's but cost twice as much. If they both do the same job, why pay more?

Although it may appear that they do the same job, it's like comparing a mini pickup with a full-sized truck. Yes, both of them can haul a set amount, but which one will hold up better working day in and day out? The full-sized truck, of course, since it's built with a heavy workload in mind and engineered for every-day use (and abuse).

Stationary planers are similarly designed for heavy-duty use. Besides using a powerful induction motor instead of the weaker universal type, the internal parts of a quality stationary planer are beefier, often heavy cast iron and machined to close tolerances.

Sure, you can surface 100 board feet of oak with a bench-top planer, but it'll take long and will take its toll on the machine. A stationary planer, on the other hand, wouldn't bat an eye at 1,000 board feet. Stationary planers, with their serrated metal infeed rollers, are the best choice if you're planning on surfacing rough-sawn lumber. The rubber infeed rollers on portable planers just don't afford as good a grip and often stall, causing burning.

ANATOMY OF A STATIONARY PLANER

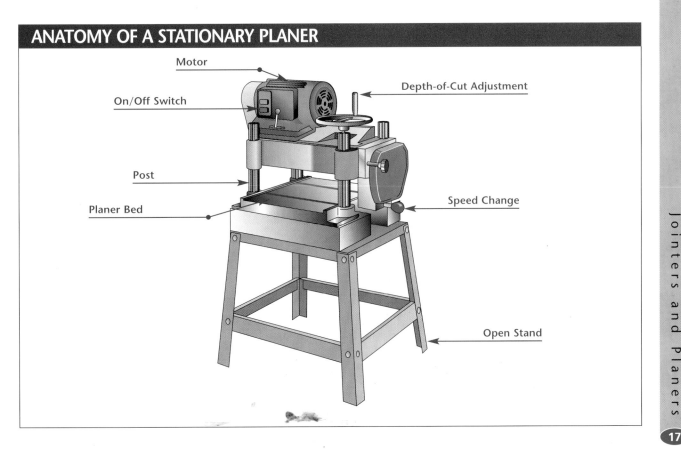

Motor

On/Off Switch

Depth-of-Cut Adjustment

Post

Planer Bed

Speed Change

Open Stand

PLANER FEATURES

Bed Width Bed width is an important consideration when you're looking for a planer. As I mentioned previously, you can find both bench-top planers and stationary planers with similar capacities. Shown here are two Jet planers: a 13" planer/molder (*left in photo*) and a 12½" bench-top planer (*right in photo*). Here again, although the width capacity is similar, the stationary jointer will hold up much better under heavy use. Most serious home woodworkers opt for a 15" stationary planer, although you can find these up to the staggering width of 48".

Thickness Capacity Thickness capacity is also a concern, but less so, as even small bench-top planers can handle up to 6"-thick stock (*see the planer at right in the photo*). Most woodworkers find this more than adequate for their home shop. Larger stationary planers often have capacities of 8" and greater, but 6" is also common (*see the planer at left in the photo*).

Motor Size Motor size is fair indication of the planer's power. For universal motors (*like the one shown here*), ignore the horsepower rating and look for the amperage rating of the motor (in this case, 15 amps). Generally, the higher the amperage, the more powerful the motor. The horsepower ratings on induction motors are fairly accurate, but check the label for the wiring class of the motor—it should at least be a "B" ("F" is superior). Many import motors are not rated at all or have the lowest class ("A"). A motor with a poor wiring class will overheat quickly and need to be replaced.

Stand/Portability Just as with jointers, the stand for a planer can have a large impact on its performance. Look for a stand that's both heavy and well constructed, as this will help dampen vibration (*see page 27 for more on planer stands*).

If portability is an issue with a stationary planer, choose a stand with wheels that lock, like those *shown in the photo at left*. For the utmost in stability, make sure that all of the wheels lock, not just one set of wheels.

Infeed and Outfeed Tables Another important feature, and one that's often overlooked, is the type of infeed/outfeed tables. There are three common types: solid tables (like the Delta planer *at left in the photo*), tables with rollers (Jet planer *at right in photo*), and rollers-only (*see the stationary planer on page 17*). Which type you choose depends on your preference—I prefer solid tables on bench-top planers, and rollers-only on stationary models. Whichever type you choose, just make sure that it's easy to adjust them up and down for proper alignment (*see page 98 for more on this*).

Knife Changing Just as with a jointer, changing knives on a planer can be a hassle. With this in mind, it's worth the time to investigate the knife-changing procedure for the planer(s) you have in mind. Some of the bench-top planer manufacturers have gone to double-sided disposable knives that can be flipped when one side dulls and then thrown away when both are dull. Replacement blades are fairly inexpensive and often very easy to replace. The knives in stationary planers are often spring-loaded and are best changed with the aid of a magnetic setting jig (*see page 101*).

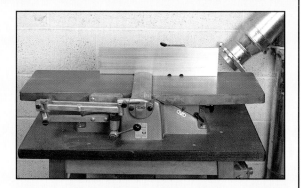

Jointer/Planer

My first shop was the second bedroom in a single-wide mobile home—tiny, to say the least. With such limited space, I took a hard look at multipurpose machines. One of the first tools I purchased was the Inca jointer *shown at top right.* Granted, it had a short bed; but it fit my space, the bed was wide (8⅝"), and it came with an optional "thicknessing" attachment (*see the photo at right, second from top*).

The thicknessing attachment slipped onto the infeed table and did a surprisingly good job—although it didn't have a power feed. Instead, it relied on good old muscle power to feed the stock through. I built a lot of furniture with this machine and still use the jointer for smaller projects. A number of manufacturers continue to sell jointer/planers, most often in an "over and under" configuration, where the jointer on top and the planer below share a common cutterhead.

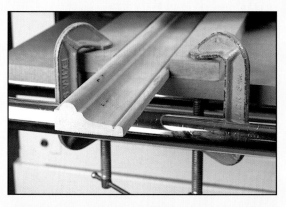

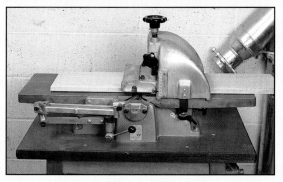

Planer/Molder

Another nifty multipurpose machine that can save you space is a planer/molder, like the Jet unit *shown in the photos at lower right.* It combines the functions of a stationary planer and a shaper (or molder). Although not as versatile as a shaper, it can produce an amazing array of molded profiles—everything from crown molding to tongue-and-groove flooring.

The way it works is, there's a section in the middle of the cutterhead where you can remove a set of spacers and replace these with molding cutters (*see the photo at bottom right*). (Note: Wide cutters require that the knives be removed entirely.). A shop-made bed with guide rails is attached to the bed of the planer, and the stock is fed through. If you have limited space and wish to make your own molding, a planer/molder is right for you.

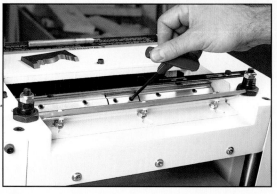

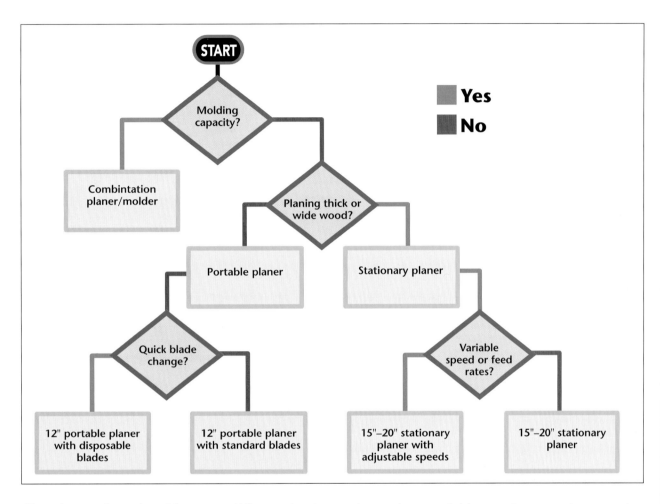

Choosing a planer is a bit more complicated than selecting a jointer, as there are more choices involved. The first step again is looking at what type of work you expect to do. If you're planning on surfacing rough-sawn lumber, go with a stationary planer and make sure it has a serrated metal infeed roller. Also, if your woodworking requires a lot of planing, you'll be better served with a stationary planer.

When going to purchase a larger machine, consider investing in at least a 15" planer with a large dust-collection port (5" to 6" diameter) and a closed base.

If you work primarily with surfaced wood and your woodworking is limited to nights and weekends (like most of us), a quality bench-top planer will get the job done. Look for a model with adjustable infeed/outfeed tables, a strong motor, easy-to-adjust controls, and disposable knives that are simple to change or replace. Also, new advances in planer design have greatly reduced snipe—look for this when you shop.

2 JOINTER AND PLANER ACCESSORIES

Unlike most power tools that have a gaggle of accessories that you can buy, jointers and planers don't have nearly as many. Part of this has to do with the simplicity of both tools and with the fact that each tool is primarily designed to do a single task, and to do that task well. The few accessories that you can purchase for a planer or jointer are important in terms of both safety and precision. With this in mind, it's a good idea to thoroughly research each of the accessories to make sure that you end up with quality accessories that will get the job done.

In this chapter, I'll start by going over one of the most important safety accessories you can purchase for a jointer: a push block. Push blocks not only can save your fingers, they also add precision to your jointing operations by ensuring that the workpiece is held firmly against the table as it passes over the cutterhead (*opposite page*).

Next, I'll go over stands for jointers. I realize that these aren't very glamorous, but they do impact on the performance of the jointer and are worth a close look (*page 24*).

Although you'll most likely only ever use HSS (high-speed steel) knives in your jointer or planer, it's worthwhile to know about the other options, like carbide-tipped and solid-carbide knives, so that you can decide whether they're right for your type of work (*page 25*).

Another accessory that you'll find extremely useful for your jointer or planer is a knife-setting jig. There are numerous types out there, including a magnetic knife-setting jig, and my favorite, the dial indicator; *see page 26* for more on each of these.

Just as with jointers, the stand for a planer can impact on its performance; *see page 27* for more on the advantages and disadvantages of the different types.

Next, I'll describe the various styles of outfeed or support rollers that you can use to help support long stock and prevent snipe on either a jointer or planer (*page 28*). One of my favorite accessories for a planer, dial calipers, is described on *page 29*. Using this tool is the fastest, most accurate way to find the thickness of stock.

Finally, there's an in-depth look at some jigs available for sharpening jointer and planer knives—everything from a simple in-place honing jig to a professional-level sharpening system that creates precise, razor-sharp edges (*pages 30–31*).

In addition to the pivoting guard that comes standard on every jointer, a push block is the next most important safety device. Some savvy manufacturers are now including a set with every jointer—that's because they know all too well how dangerous an exposed cutterhead can be.

It's just a lot safer to run a board over a cutterhead with a safety barrier (the push block) between your hand and the workpiece. Let's face it, accidents do happen in the shop. One way to prevent a nasty accident with a jointer is to use a push block whenever possible.

A fellow teacher friend of mine was going over safety procedures for the jointer for his patternmaking class. Ironically, he had just gone over the importance of using a push block before his demonstration. For reasons still unknown, he failed to use one in the demo, his hand slipped, and in a split second the tips of three fingers were gone. This wouldn't have happened if he'd followed his own advice.

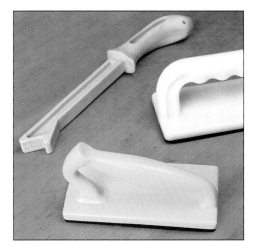

Commercial Commercially made push blocks come in a variety of shapes and sizes. The most common type resembles a grout float used for tile work. This style of push block has a rubber cushion on the bottom and does not have a lip. The gripping power is provided by the rubber face and can slip if it's not kept clean— I like to give this type of push block a quick shot of compressed air before each use. Over time, sawdust can build up, and the rubber face should be cleaned with a mild detergent solution. Although the lipped push stick *shown in the left corner of the photo* is designed for use with a table saw, it's handy for edge-jointing narrow stock.

Shop-Made The style of push block that I prefer for use on the jointer is type that has a lip (*see the photo at left*). The lip fits over the edge of the workpiece and provides a more positive grip. I've had no-lip push blocks slip on me before, and I didn't care for the experience at all. The push block *shown here* is easy to make and will serve you well for years. *See pages 62–63 for detailed directions on how to make it.*

JOINTER STANDS

Open Base As I mentioned in Chapter 1, the base or stand of a jointer can have a big impact on the jointer's performance. The heavier it is, and the sturdier the construction, the better it can dampen vibration. The open base stand *shown here* is my last choice for a stand for a couple of reasons.

First, although it's fairly sturdy, it doesn't weigh much. And more importantly, this type of stand does not lend itself well to dust collection. However, this stand does offer storage space (the lower shelf), which closed base stands don't.

Closed Base A sturdy, closed base stand like the one *shown in the photo at right* provides both a solid foundation for the jointer and a quick and easy way to control and convey dust and chips. To hook the jointer up to a dust collector, all you need to do is attach a pick-up to the dust chute and connect this via flexible hose to your collector.

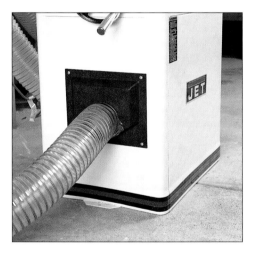

An added benefit of a closed base is that it shields the motor from collecting shop dust. Fine dust like this can penetrate into the bearings and coat the windings—which can shorten the life of the motor.

Shop-Made An alternative to buying a closed base stand is to build one yourself. The shop-made stand *shown here* is constructed out of ¾" MDF (medium-density fiberboard). Since this material is dense and heavy (about 100 pounds per sheet) and this stand uses most of a sheet, it does a good job of dampening vibration. This stand also features a pull-out chip bin that contains and collects chips for removal. (For step-by-step instructions on how to make this stand, *see pages 64–67.*)

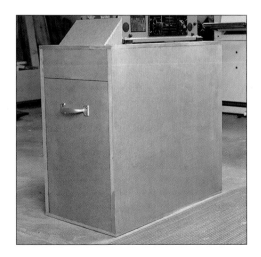

Jointer and Planer Accessories

HSS Virtually every jointer you buy will come with a set of HSS (high-speed steel) knives. These knives will perform admirably in most shop situations, they can be resharpened, and they'll last for years.

Jointer and planer knives are available in a huge variety of widths and lengths, with or without mounting holes or slots (*see the photo at left*). If you need to purchase replacement knives, it's best to buy them from the original manufacturer to ensure that they're the correct size and type.

Carbide-Tipped For a longer-lasting edge, you might want to consider a set of carbide-tipped knives. This type of knife is an HSS body with a length of carbide permanently bonded to the tip (*see the photo at left*). This style of knife is less brittle than a solid-carbide knife (*see below*) and is much less expensive. Carbide-tipped knives typically cost 20% to 40% more than the HSS knives. Although they do hold an edge longer, they nick more easily and are much more costly to have sharpened.

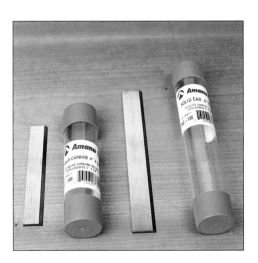

Carbide Since solid-carbide knives are expensive—roughly 50% to 60% more than HSS knives—they're not for everyone. Just as with carbide-tipped knives, they'll hold an edge longer; but since the entire knife is carbide, they can be resharpened many more times than a carbide-tipped knife. If you're working with a lot of highly abrasive woods (like teak, ebony, or osage orange), a set of solid-carbide knives may be worth the investment. Otherwise, I recommend sticking with HSS or carbide-tipped knives.

Jointers and Planers

25

KNIFE-SETTING JIGS

Magnetic Jointer Knife Jigs Since changing and adjusting jointer knives can be a hassle, a number of tool accessory manufacturers have come up with jigs to make the job easier. The most common of these is a magnetic knife-setting jig like the one *shown in the photo at right.*

This style of jig uses two sets of powerful magnets: one to attach to the jointer bed, the other to hold the knives in perfect position so that you can tighten the mounting bolts or screws. Most of these will work on jointers with knives up to 8" in width, regardless of the diameter of the cutterhead.

Magnetic Planer Knife Jigs Because of cramped spaces, I find planer knives even more of a hassle to adjust than jointer knives. Fortunately, tool accessory manufacturers came to the rescue with magnetic knife-setting jigs for planers, like the ones *shown in the photo at right.*

It's important to note that these knife-setting jigs are designed for specific diameter cutterheads—the ones *shown here* can handle most portable planers but are too small for the larger diameter head of a stationary planer.

Dial Indicator My favorite tool for adjusting jointer knives is a dial indicator like the one *shown in the photo at right.* Fitted with a magnetic base that holds it securely to your jointer bed, you can use it to make knife-height measurement in increments of one thousandth of an inch (0.001"). This super-accurate tool is the ultimate way to precisely set the height of the knives. (For detailed instructions on using a dial indicator, *see page 91.*)

The same features that describe well-made jointer stands—heavy and sturdy—apply to planer stands. But unlike jointer stands, where a closed base is best, planers will work equally well with an open or a closed base. That's because dust and chip collection isn't an issue for the stand. The reason is that chips and dust are collected from planers from above. In most cases a dust port or hood is attached directly to or over the planer head and is then connected to a dust collector via a flexible hose.

With this in mind, selecting an open or closed base is really a matter of personal preference. For the most part, woodworkers who have other machines with closed bases tend to stick with closed bases, more for looks than anything else. Here again, the advantage of an open base is that it often affords more storage space—you could easily add a lower shelf to the shop-made stand *shown below.*

Commercial Most tool manufacturers offer both closed and open bases for their tools. For stationary planers (like the one *shown in the photo at left*), a closed base may be a better choice. That's because it encloses the motor and keeps dust and chips from penetrating the bearings and coating the windings—both of which can shorten the life expectancy of the motor. Closed bases often weigh more than the equivalent open stand and will therefore dampen vibration better.

Shop-Made Shop-made stands are an alternative to buying one. If you decide to build one, stick with heavy materials (like MDF) and use sturdy construction—like the mortise-and-tenon base *shown here.* Because of its open base style, you can add a shelf below for storage. This stand also features table extensions to help support long stock and prevent snipe. For step-by-step directions on how to build this planer stand, *see pages 72–75.*

OUTFEED ROLLERS

Regardless of the length of a workpiece, if it's not supported properly, it can tilt or pivot up or down so that the cutterhead ends up gouging the workpiece. This incident is referred to as "snipe" and is extremely common when working with planers and an occasional problem with a jointer. One way to help prevent this from happening in either case is to support the workpiece fully throughout the entire cut—here's where outfeed or support rollers come to the rescue. As the name implies, outfeed rollers are most commonly used on the outfeed side of a machine, but they can also serve well on the infeed side—particularly when you're working with long boards.

Although any solid table at roughly the same height as the planer or jointer bed will do to support the workpiece, rollers work best because they provide frictionless support. And the more rollers, the better since they will support a longer portion of the workpiece and help prevent it from dipping or twisting.

Commercial Commercially made rollers like the one *shown in the photo at right* can be purchased for under $40. They are adjustable in height over a fairly wide range and can be used to support stock when you're operating a wide variety of tools. While rollers like the one *shown here* do a reasonable job of supporting stock, I prefer a more stable base and multiple rollers like the shop-made stand *shown below.*

Shop-Made For less than 20 bucks, you can build a better outfeed roller than you can buy for a lot more money. The shop-made roller *shown here* features four rollers and a sturdy base. The height of the rollers is adjustable to support stock on most machines. The rollers are made from scraps of PVC pipe and some toy wheels. For complete directions on how to make this outfeed table, *see pages 80–83.*

DIAL CALIPERS

If you don't own a dial caliper, buy one. I realize that this is a pretty strong statement, but you'll be glad you did. Using a dial caliper is one of the most accurate ways to precisely measure the thickness of stock—and they're incredibly easy to use.

I started using a dial caliper about 15 years ago and have used one on just about every project I've built since then. If you've ever struggled with a metal ruler or a tape measure, trying to measure the thickness of a workpiece accurately, you'll really appreciate one of these nifty tools.

Dial calipers are available with either metal or plastic bodies. Even though the metal bodies are typically more accurate, I prefer the plastic bodies for a couple of reasons. First, they're less likely to mar the wood. And second, they're less expensive. I've found the plastic dial calipers to be more than accurate for everyday use.

Close the jaws on the workpiece. Using a dial caliper is simplicity itself. Just slide open the jaws of the caliper, insert the workpiece, and slide the jaws tightly closed. Make sure the jaws are in complete contact with the workpiece to get the most accurate reading.

Most dial calipers also feature a metal rod that protrudes from the end of the body. This rod is useful for taking accurate depth measurements. Just butt the end of the body against the lip of a hole or depression, slide open the jaws until the rod strikes the bottom, and then read the dial.

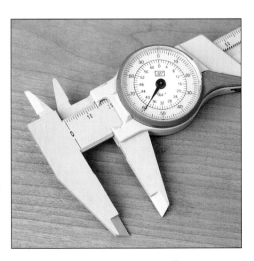

Dial is easy to read. Although a dail caliper is not as accurate as a micrometer, it's a whole lot easier to read. Most are calibrated in hundredths and/or 64ths of an inch—plenty accurate for even the most discriminating woodworker.

When shopping for a dial caliper, look for one that's calibrated in both hundredths and 64ths of an inch. Be careful—many of these read in hundredths of an inch only. And even though they often have a conversion chart on the body of the caliper or its case, that type is a hassle to use. Stick with a caliper with 64ths clearly labeled on the dial face.

Jointers and Planers

KNIFE-SHARPENING JIGS

As with any edged tool, the knives in a planer or jointer will eventually dull with use and need to be resharpened. There are two basic methods for handling this task. If the knives are in reasonable shape (no nicks or severely blunted edges), it may be possible to hone them in place with a sharpening stone; *see the jig below.* Please note that honing doesn't replace sharpening; it simply lengthens the time required between sharpenings.

To sharpen jointer or planer knives, you'll first need to remove them. There are a couple of sharpening jigs on the market for jointer knifes up to 8" in width (*see below*); but unless you've got a specialty sharpening system (like the Tormek system *shown on the opposite page*) that can handle the longer planer knives (10" and over), you'll need to drop off your planer knives at a sharpening service. Ask your woodworking buddies or the local guild for recommendations for a sharpening service if you haven't used one before.

Honing in Place There are a couple of honing jigs available for quickly bringing up a fresh edge on your jointer or planer knives. The one *shown here* has two different shaped stones embedded in a wooden holder. The square stone is used to lap the back of the knife and the other stone is beveled to match the angle of the knives. When using one of these, make sure that the knives are clean and that the machine is unplugged prior to sharpening.

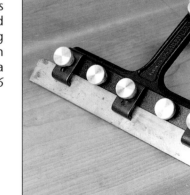

Veritas Jig The jointer knife sharpener *shown here* is manufactured by Veritas and does a great job of holding jointer knives at a precise angle for sharpening. Since most oilstones and whetstones are not large enough to handle an 8" knife, the jig comes with a pressure-sensitive sheet of micro-abrasive that can be mounted to any flat surface—the bed of your jointer or a piece of ¼"-thick tempered glass works well. *See pages 95–96* for step-by-step instructions on how to use this handy jig.

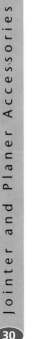

TORMEK SHARPENING SYSTEM

The first time I saw a Tormek sharpening system demonstrated, I was really impressed at how easy it was to create a professional edge on almost any cutting tool. The Tormek system is a water-cooled grinding unit that allows for both fast and slow cutting action on the same wheel; *see the photo at right.* Since it's water-cooled, there's no risk of overheating a knife or blade and causing it to lose its temper. But what really make the Tormek system unique are the numerous tool-holding jigs available that guarantee precise angles coupled with repeatable grinds. The big advantage to a repeatable grind is that once you've ground the tool to the exact angle and shape, you have to remove only a tiny bit of material on subsequent sharpenings. This means the knives or blades will last longer.

The only drawback to this system is its cost. The system plus the jointer/planer knife-sharpening jig will run you over $500. Granted, you can get a lot of knives sharpened for that, but if you do invest in one of these, you'll find that you'll use it for all your tools. (Note: There's even a universal gouge jig that will allow you to grind flawless bevels on difficult-to-sharpen tools like bowl gouges and carving tools.) You could even sharpen knives and tools for your woodworking friends for a modest fee to defray the cost of the tool.

The bottom line here is, this is the only sharpening system I've seen for home woodworkers that can handle long jointer and planer knives. Here's how the system works. You start by clamping the knife in the holder. Then the holder is placed on the support and the grinding length is adjusted (*see the middle drawing at right*). Next you adjust the edge angle by turning a knob, and all that's left is to set the grinding depth and grind (*see the bottom photo at right*).

Photos and drawing courtesy of Tormek, © 2001

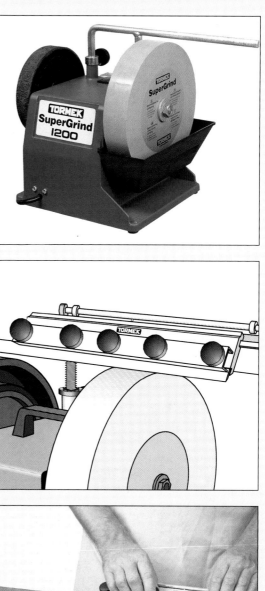

3 BASIC OPERATIONS

Although the basic operations of jointing and planing are fairly straightforward, it is imperative to the success of your woodworking to use the proper technique. I can't tell you how many intermediate (and even some advanced) woodworkers I've seen use poor jointing or planing technique.

For example, many of them will press down a workpiece only on the infeed table side of a jointer, when the downward pressure should shift to the outfeed table after the workpiece passes over the cutterhead. Or some folks use a planer without infeed or outfeed support and then complain about snipe.

Proper jointing and planing techniques are so important because they create the foundation for the rest of your work by creating square stock. Without these fundamental building blocks, a project is doomed to turn out less than satisfactory.

In this chapter, I'll start by going over a simple routine to set up your jointer for work (*opposite page*). Then I'll take you through the techniques for edge-jointing (*page 34*) and face-jointing (*page 35*)—everything from proper grain direction to the different types of push blocks and when to use them.

Next, there's information on how to handle some specialty cuts with the jointer, like jointing end grain, plywood, or veneer (*see page 36 for more on this*). It's also important to know how to safely handle short and long stock (*page 37*) and how to remove cup or warp from a board (*page 38*).

Then it's on to using a planer. I'll begin with planer setup (*page 39*) and move on to basic technique (*pages 40–41*), including a way to make staggered cuts to prevent snipe.

Next is the all-important recommended sequence for squaring up stock (*pages 42–43*). If you religiously follow this sequence (and your tools are properly adjusted), you'll end up with square, flat stock—a real pleasure to work with.

Finally, there's a short section on how to use portable power planers: everything from setting one up, to cutting rabbets, bevels, and chamfers.

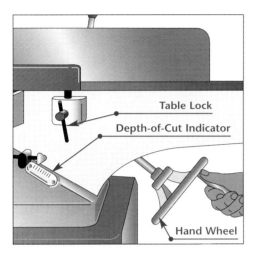

Table Lock

Depth-of-Cut Indicator

Hand Wheel

1 Set depth of cut The first thing you'll need to do to set up a jointer for use is to set the depth of cut. Start by loosening the infeed table lock (*shown in the drawing directly above the depth-of-cut indicator*), and then turn the hand wheel or adjust the lever to move the infeed table up or down as desired (see your owner's manual for the maximum recommended cut). Note that though most jointers will have a depth-of-cut gauge, they serve only as a rough estimate of how much stock will be removed. Once the depth is set, retighten the table lock.

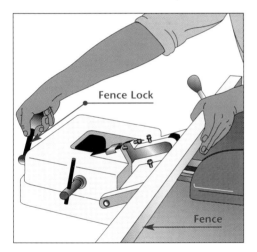

Fence Lock

Fence

2 Adjust fence The next step is to adjust the position and/or angle of the jointer fence. Loosen the fence lock (*as shown*) and slide the fence into the desired position and retighten the lock. **ShopTip:** It's a good idea to routinely move the position of the fence over the entire width of the table so that the full width of the knives gets used. If you don't, and you do a lot of edge-jointing, the small area next to the fence will get dull. Then when you go to face-joint a piece, you'll get an uneven cut.

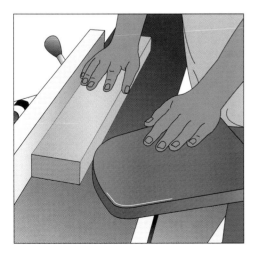

3 Check guard The final step before jointing is to check to make sure that the guard is set up and functioning properly. Do this by sliding the workpiece past the knives with the power off. Check that the guard swings easily out of the way, yet still maintains contact with the workpiece—and that no portion of the knives are exposed. If you can see knives, stop and adjust the guard, replace the spring, or do whatever is necessary to correct this dangerous fault.

Jointers and Planers

EDGE-JOINTING

Grain Direction Regardless of the jointing operation, to get the smoothest cut, you must take into account the grain direction of the workpiece. For the best overall cut, the grain should slope down and away from the cutterhead, *as shown in the drawing at right.*

In a perfect world, this is always possible. But any woodworker knows that grain can switch direction in a piece—often multiple times. In cases like this, try to joint the piece so the majority of the grain is sloping down and away—and take a very light cut.

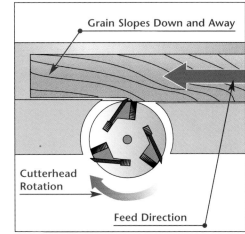

1 Start the cut Edge-jointing is a fairly straightforward operation, as long as you follow a couple of simple rules. First, make sure to press the workpiece firmly into the side of the fence at all times in order to achieve a perpendicular cut. Second, position the workpiece a few inches away from the cutterhead and slowly feed the workpiece past the guard. As the workpiece crosses the cutterhead, shift your weight to the outfeed table.

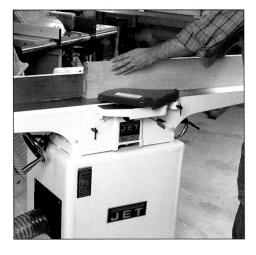

2 Finish the cut It's a common misconception of many woodworkers that you should press down heavily on the infeed table. Although you should press down some here, the bulk of the pressure should always be on the outfeed table. That's why it's important to shift your weight to the outfeed side as soon as the workpiece passes the cutterhead, *as shown in the photo at right.*

Push Block The number one rule for face-jointing is: Never pass your hand directly over the cutterhead. The problem with this is that you need to apply downward pressure to the workpiece as it passes over the cutterhead. The solution is to use some form of push block. The lipped push block *shown here* works well for pushing the workpiece ahead, but it doesn't do much for downward pressure.

Grout Floats Since grout float–style push blocks don't have a lip, they work extremely well for applying pressure to the workpiece as it passes over the cutterhead; *see the photo at left.* This is important to get an even cut and prevents the workpiece from "chattering" (bouncing as it comes in contact with the cutterhead) and producing a ribbed cut.

The disadvantage to grout float–style push blocks is that they can slip during the cut. The best method I've found is to use a lipped push block to guide the workpiece and a float-style push block for downward pressure.

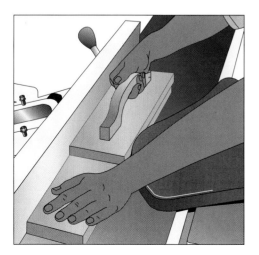

Basic Technique The basic technique for face-jointing is as follows. Use a push block to guide the workpiece into the cutterhead. If you have a grout float–style push block, set it directly over the end of the workpiece, and apply downward pressure as it engages the cutterhead and passes onto the outfeed table. Allow the workpiece to slide under it as you continue to apply pressure just past the cutterhead directly over the outfeed table. If you're using hand pressure, allow the first 6" of the workpiece to pass the cutterhead before applying downward pressure, *as shown.*

SPECIALTY JOINTER CUTS

Jointing End Grain Even though most woodworkers would never consider jointing end grain, it's quite doable, as long as your knives are sharp and you take a light cut. The only worry is chip-out as you complete the cut. There are two methods to prevent this.

The first method (*shown here*) is to clamp a sacrificial scrap piece to the end of the workpiece and joint as usual. The other method is a little trickier: Start jointing the end grain, and then stop after about 2" to 3". Then flip the workpiece end for end and finish the cut. Be careful not to go past the previously jointed end grain, or it may chip out.

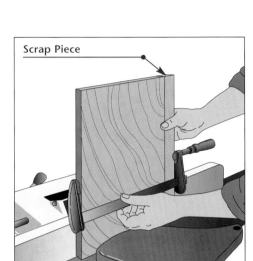

Scrap Piece

Plywood Jointing plywood is another one of those procedures that makes most woodworkers shudder. But here again, it's quite easy to do as long as you take light cuts and your knives are sharp. Why would you want to joint plywood? I've often done it on the edges of shelves on which I was planning to glue a strip to conceal the edge. The cleaner the edge, the better the glue joint. One thing to keep in mind: Plywood does contain a high glue content, which can act as an abrasive, dulling knives—so use this technique sparingly.

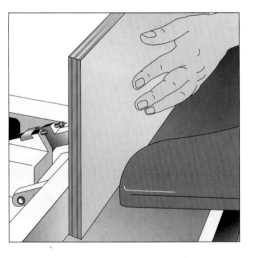

Veneer A final specialty cut that is a real problem solver is jointing the edges of veneer or laminate in order to get a perfect glue joint. To do this, just sandwich the pieces of veneer or laminate to be joined between two layers of plywood or other straight stock (*see the drawing at right*). Position the veneer or laminate so it barely sticks out along its entire length on the bottom. Then take a series of light cuts until you've exposed fresh wood along the full length of the veneer and plywood scraps.

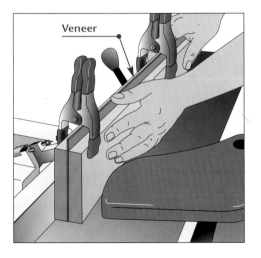

Veneer

Anyone that's ever bought a power tool and looked through the owner's manual knows that the first couple of pages are devoted to various types of warnings. Most of these are commonsense, and sadly, many of them are ignored.

Although they're all important, there's one special warning that I'd like to emphasize. And that's the minimum stock length that can be safely jointed. Small bench-top jointers typically have a minimum length around 10"; on larger jointers it's usually around 14". Don't try to joint pieces shorter than this! More jointer accidents occur because of trying to joint short pieces than for any other reason. Read and heed the manufacturer's recommendations.

Working with long stock can also be dangerous, as an unsupported workpiece can get away from you. The solution is to use some type of infeed or outfeed support, or both (*see below*).

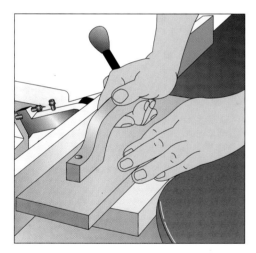

Short Stock OK, so let's assume that you need to joint some short stock that's over the minimum required length. Rule #1: No matter whether you're edge-jointing or face-jointing, use a push block. Rule #2: Keep your other hand and fingers away from the cutterhead. Don't be tempted to apply downward pressure to the workpiece with your fingers *as shown in the drawing at left;* instead, center the push block on the workpiece and keep both hands on it. Rule #3: Take light, slow cuts.

Long Stock Trying to joint long stock on a short-bed jointer (*like the one shown in the photo at left*) without using some form of support is an accident waiting to happen. The weight of an unsupported workpiece can tilt the piece up, exposing the cutterhead at either the beginning or the end of the cut. To prevent this, position one (or better yet, two) support rollers on each end of the jointer to fully support the workpiece through the entire cut.

Jointers and Planers

37

REMOVING CUP WITH THE JOINTER

One of the most common mistakes I've seen wood-workers make when using a planer is to try flattening cupped or warped stock with just the planer alone. Granted, you will get a thicknessed board with parallel faces—the problem is, the cup or warp will most likely still be there.

The reason for this is that the infeed and outfeed rollers of the planer are typically strong enough to hold the board flat as it passes under the cutter-head. But as soon as the board is free from this pressure, it'll spring back to its original form.

The way to get around this is to remove the cup or warp on one face with the jointer and then place the flattened face on the bed of the planer to serve as a reference for the other face. This method creates smooth, flat boards without cup or warp. (For more on the correct sequence for squaring stock, *see pages 42–43*.)

1 Flatten concave face The first step in removing cup is to place the workpiece on the jointer with the concave face down, *as shown in the drawing at right.* Set the jointer for a light cut (around ¹⁄₁₆") and, using push blocks, pass the workpiece slowly over the cutterhead. Don't worry about keeping the edge of the board perfectly flush with the fence—you can joint a perpendicular edge after you've jointed the face flat. Take as many light passes as necessary until the face is flat. **ShopTip**: Scribble a light pencil mark across the face of the board—when it's completely gone, the face is flat.

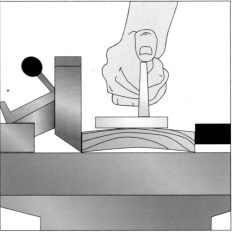

2 Flatten opposite face If possible, the preferred method for getting a parallel flat face is to run the board through a planer once one face is flat. If you don't have access to a planer, you can get a fairly parallel face with the jointer alone. Start by jointing one edge perpendicular to the flattened face. Then position the workpiece with the concave face down and with the jointed edge against the fence (*see the drawing at right*). The key thing here is to keep the jointed edge absolutely flush with the fence to prevent the board from rocking as you cut. Take light cuts and go slowly here.

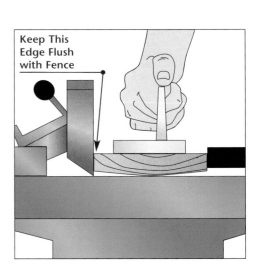

Keep This Edge Flush with Fence

1 Align the support table or rollers Whenever I'm getting ready to plane a large amount of stock, I start by double-checking that the support tables or rollers are aligned with the bed of the planer. To do this, I place an accurate straightedge on edge on the bed of the planer so that it extends out onto the support table or rollers, *as shown in the photo at left.* Then I adjust the table or rollers up or down until they're flush with the bottom edge of the straightedge. This is one of the simplest ways to help prevent snipe (*for more on this, see page 121*).

2 Adjust the depth of cut Once you're sure the planer's support tables or rollers are aligned, the next step is to adjust the depth of cut. If you're planing rough-sawn wood, insert a scrap piece into the planer and then lower the head (or raise the table) until the cutterhead contacts the scrap. This gives you an idea of where to start. Then back off the cut a quarter turn to release the scrap, and adjust for the depth of cut desired. Here again, consult the owner's manual for maximum cut; as always, lighter cuts will produce a smoother overall cut and be easier on the planer.

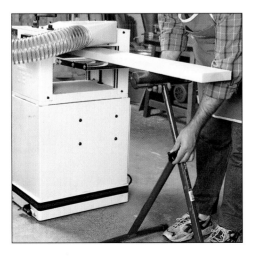

3 Add outfeed support Unless you're planing fairly short stock (make sure the pieces are longer than the recommended minimum width), you'll need to add some form of support to either the infeed, the outfeed, or both. Position a roller support as needed, and adjust its height so that it's just a hair lower than the planer's support tables or rollers. If you adjust it to the same height as the roller, the workpiece can catch the side of the roller instead of passing over it.

Jointers and Planers

BASIC PLANER TECHNIQUE

Surfacing wood on a properly adjusted and finely tuned planer is simply a matter of feeding the stock in one end and lifting it out the other. In a perfect world, snipe does not exist. In the real world, it's a fact of life. Although many woodworkers resign themselves to always having snipe, there are ways to minimize and even prevent this from happening.

What's surprising is that snipe can be minimized and/or prevented with the proper technique; *see below.* Sure, if the planer's not adjusted properly and the workpiece isn't supported, snipe will occur no matter what you do in terms of technique. But if you follow the planing procedure *described below and on the next page,* you'll be pleasantly surprised by the outcome.

1 Start the cut Once you've set up your planer and have adjusted it for the desired depth of cut, you're ready to plane. Whenever possible, hook the planer up to a dust collection system. This helps keep chips and dust off the infeed and outfeed rollers so that they can grip the workpiece efficiently. Place one end of the board on the planer bed, lower the opposite end until it's almost level, and feed it slowly into the planer until the infeed roller takes over. A slight lift to the board will help prevent snipe as it contacts the cutterhead. In no case should the end of the board slant down, or else a huge snipe will result.

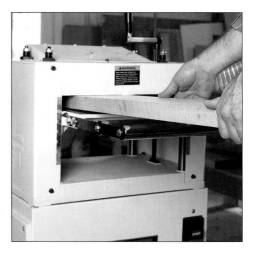

2 Push as a last resort If the feed rollers on a planer are adjusted properly, you should never have to push the workpiece into the planer—the rollers should grip and move it through at the correct speed. This is especially true when the feed rollers are the serrated metal variety. This type of roller affords a much better grip on the workpiece than the rubber variety, particularly on rough-sawn lumber. If the planer bogs down and the workpiece pauses, you may be trying to take too deep of a cut. Before resorting to pushing, try adjusting for a lighter cut—the rollers may then be able to do their job.

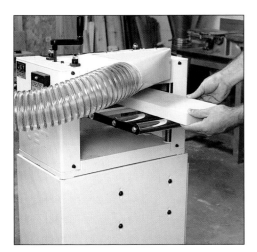

3 Pull if you must Just as with pushing, you shouldn't have to pull a board through a planer. Admittedly, this is required sometimes, particularly with wide stock on a planer with rubber rollers. The rollers just can't grip the board sufficiently to push it past the cutterhead while it's trying to remove a lot of wood. Keeping rubber rollers clean will help, but making light cuts is the best way to avoid a tug-of-war with your planer.

4 Lift to prevent snipe Since snipe most often occurs at the end of a planer's cut, one simple way to reduce it is to *gently* lift the end of the board up as it nears the end of the cut, *as shown in the photo at left.* In effect what you're doing here is applying some leverage to the board (via the outfeed roller) to offset the natural tendency of the board to lift up once its end is free from the downward pressure applied by the infeed roller. The key here is gentle pressure; if you lift up hard and often, you'll end up weakening the springs on the outfeed roller.

STAGGERED CUTS

Here's a slick way to avoid snipe when you're planing multiple pieces that are the same thickness. **Safety Note:** You should use this technique only when all the pieces are the identical thickness—if some are thinner, they won't be captured by the rollers and could kick back when they come in contact with the cutterhead. The way this works is simple. By having the stock pieces fed into the planer so they're staggered (*as shown in the photo*), the infeed and outfeed rollers are constantly under tension, just as if you were planing a long board. Since snipe occurs only at the start or finish of a cut, it can occur only on the first and last pieces fed into the planer.

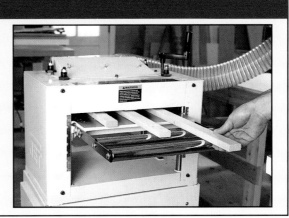

WOODWORKING SUCCESSS STARTS WITH SQUARE STOCK

Although the sequence shown here for squaring up stock is no secret, it is one of the foundations to successful woodworking. If you don't start with square stock, virtually nothing else you do with the stock will work out right. Joinery won't fit, you'll experience gaps in your glue joints, and your projects won't hold up well over time.

Although I've said it previously, it bears repeating: None of the wood you buy will be perfectly square or flat. Just because a board is surfaced on all four sides doesn't mean it's square. Most likely it will be thicknessed accurately, but it won't be flat or square. The only way to ensure it is for you to make it so. The sequence *shown here* is the quickest, easiest way to get square stock for your woodworking projects.

1 Face-joint The first step in squaring up stock is to joint one face smooth (*see the photo at right*). Use a push block (or two), and press the workpiece firmly against the infeed and outfeed tables as you make the cut. Remember never to pass your hands directly over the cutterhead, and to shift your weight to the outfeed table once the stock has passed the cutterhead. Don't worry about keeping the edge perfectly flush with the fence—you'll clean it up in the next step.

2 Edge-joint After one face is jointed flat, the next step to squaring stock is to joint an edge perpendicular to the flattened face. Press the jointed face up firmly against the fence, and take a series of light cuts until the entire edge is jointed flat (*see the photo at right*). Here again, you'll want to shift your weight to the outfeed table once the stock passes over the cutterhead.

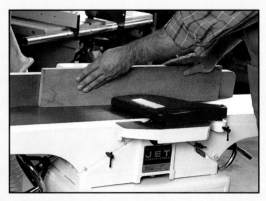

3 Thickness-plane Now that you have two flat perpendicular edges, you can create two flat parallel faces. The best tool for the job here is the planer. Place the flattened face against the bed of the planer, adjust for a light cut, and feed the board into the planer (*see the photo at left*). Let the infeed roller take over and push the board past the cutterhead. When it comes out the other side, lift the end of the board lightly to help prevent snipe.

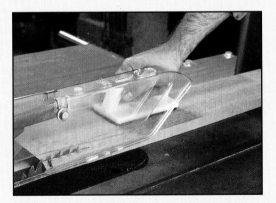

4 Rip the remaining edge With three square, flat sides, all that's left is to square up the remaining edge. In most cases, you'll want to rip the board to rough width on the table saw (*see the photo at left*). Then follow this up with a light pass or two over the jointer to bring the board to its final width and also to remove any saw marks.

SQUARING-STOCK SEQUENCE

Joint One Face

Joint Adjacent Edge

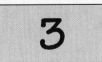

Thickness-Plane
Opposite Face

Rip to Width

USING A PORTABLE POWER PLANER

Depth of Cut The first thing to do with a power planer is to adjust it to the desired depth of cut. As always, I'd recommend taking a series of lighter cuts instead of one heavy cut. The cut of most power planers is adjusted by turning a large knob on the front of the planer to the depth indicated on the scale (*see the photo at right*). Note that virtually every power planer has a "zero" or "P" (for "park") position that sets the knives up into the planer so they don't protrude at all. The knives should be in this position whenever the planer is not in use.

Fence Quality portable power planers will come with a fence that can be used with the planer to make accurate cuts and rabbets (*see the opposite page*). Using an auxiliary fence like the one *shown in the photo* is also a good way to add extra support to the planer for almost any cut. Just slide the fence into the desired position and tighten the lock knob. Then butt the fence up against the side of the workpiece and make the cut.

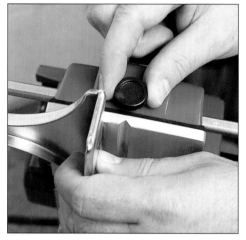

Extra Support Whenever you need to plane a narrow strip of wood, it's a good idea to add some additional support to the piece to prevent the planer from tipping sideways during the cut. The simplest way to do this is to clamp a wide scrap of wood (like the 2×4 shown here) to the side of the workpiece. This creates a stable platform for the planer, and you'll get a smoother, more accurate cut.

Cutting Rabbets One of the features I like best about a portable power planer is that it's extremely easy to cut accurate rabbets. Here's where a solid auxiliary fence comes in handy. Adjust the fence to match the desired width of the rabbet, and take a test cut on a scrap piece to make sure it's the correct width. Then adjust the planer for a light cut, and make a series of passes until the desired depth of the rabbet is reached.

Cutting Bevels Bevels are also easy to create with a power planer (*see the photo at left*). The only problem here is that since you don't have an adjustable-angle fence, you need to lay out the angle carefully on both ends of the workpiece and stop frequently to see how you're doing.

Note that even with careful layout, it's tough to cut an accurate bevel. With a little ingenuity, you may be able to fasten an angled fence to the planer to guide it for a more precise cut.

Cutting Chamfers In addition to rabbets and bevels, one of the things a power planer excels at is cutting quick chamfers. Most power planers have a groove running the length of their base designed especially for this (*see the photo at left*). This V-groove will ride along the edge of the workpiece and will press up against adjacent sides to create a very nice chamfer. This is one situation where you can safely take a deeper cut, as you're making such a narrow cut (the width of the chamfer). As always, it's a good idea to make a test cut on a scrap piece first.

C H A P T E R

4 ADVANCED OPERATIONS

Many woodworkers think of a jointer and a planer as single-purpose machines. That is, one joints edges, and the other thickness-planes. But with a little advanced knowledge and some simple jigs, you can do a lot more with both machines.

As a matter of fact, some of the techniques described in this chapter work better than the "standard" methods—especially those that are done on a table saw, which has a tendency to leave rather nasty saw marks on a workpiece.

In this chapter, I'll start by describing how to cut rabbets on the jointer (*opposite page*). This is a great way to create super-smooth rabbets fast. The only thing is, your jointer must have either a rabbeting recess on the outfeed table or else a detachable rabbeting arm.

Next, I'll show you how to taper a post on the jointer. If you've ever cut tapers on the table saw and then spent hours removing saw or burn marks, you'll really appreciate this technique. It's surprisingly simple, and it doesn't require jigs of any kind (*see pages 48–49 for more on this*).

Then I'll move on to chamfering on the jointer—a terrific way to create crisp, smooth chamfers (*page 50*). You might be surprised to learn that you can make raised panels on the jointer, all it takes is a simple shop-made sled and sharp knives (*page 51*). Another advanced technique on the jointer is the bevel. *See page 52* for more on this, including a nifty tip to guarantee precise cuts.

Tapering is also possible on the planer. It merely requires yet another shop-made sled. You can taper stock either across its width or along its length. The big advantage to tapering on the planer is that the stock comes out the perfect thickness—something that's not as easy to do on the jointer (*page 53*).

An item to note here is that planer sleds are part-specific; that is, they are built to create a specific taper on one part. Obviously it will pay off to go to the trouble to build a sled like this only if you're making multiple parts.

Finally, there's information on how to safely plane thin stock (*pages 54–55*) and how to make molding using a planer/molder (*pages 56–57*).

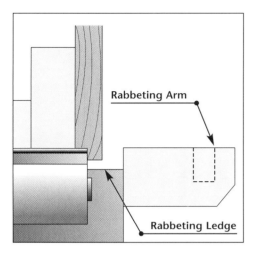

Rabbeting Arm

Rabbeting Ledge

Rabbet Some jointers have a ledge in the outfeed table or a special detachable rabbeting arm that allows for rabbeting (*see the drawing at left*). In the case of the rabbeting arm, the jointer knives will run the full length of the bed, and access to the ends of the knives is allowed by removing the arm. The disadvantage of the ledge in the outfeed table is that it limits the width of the stock that you can rabbet.

Removing the Guard Regardless of whether your jointer has a recess or a detachable arm, the first thing you'll need to do is remove the guard. **Safety Note**: Removing the guard like this exposes the knives, and extra care should be taken when using the jointer—particularly at the start and finish of the cut.

If your jointer is equipped with a rabbeting arm, remove it if you're jointing the rabbet on the face of the workpiece. Then adjust the fence over to set the rabbet width. Note that on a jointer where the fence doesn't slide over far enough, you'll need to clamp on an auxiliary fence.

Technique To joint a rabbet, start by setting the infeed table depth—odds are that you'll need to make multiple passes to achieve the desired depth. Make a trial cut on a scrap piece, and adjust the fence as necessary to get the desired width. **Safety Note**: Turn off the jointer between passes and when adjusting the infeed table, as the jointer knives are exposed. Take light cuts, and check the depth of the rabbet often.

JOINTER:
TAPERING A POST

Tapered Posts Clean, smooth tapers are easy to make on the jointer if you follow the simple procedure described here. The advantage that a jointer has over other tapering methods, especially the table saw, is that the completed leg or post requires virtually no sanding. There are no saw marks to remove—the leg is smooth and the corners are crisp (*see the photo at right*).

1 Mark the start of the taper To taper a post or leg, begin by marking a reference line on all four sides of each workpiece (*see the photo at right*). Measure down from the top to the desired starting point of the taper, and then use a try square to transfer this mark around to all four sides. You'll use these marks to position the post or leg over the cutterhead of the jointer to make the cut in Step 3.

2 Mark fence The next step is to mark a reference line on the fence of the jointer to identify the front edge of the outfeed table. Instead of marking directly on the fence, I like to add a strip of masking tape to the fence and then mark it with a pen. Now when you align the marks that you made on the post in Step 1 with the reference line on the fence, you'll know where the cut starts. Note: Instead of marking the fence at top dead-center of the cutterhead, mark it at the edge of the outfeed table to allow for a final cleanup pass to remove the dished cut the knives make.

3 **Position the post** The basic idea here is to align the marks you made on the post and the fence and then slowly and carefully lower the post onto the spinning cutterhead to start the cut. Although this may sound scary, it's really quite easy after you've practiced a bit.

ShopTip: Since most tapered posts or legs will be joined to other parts, it's best to complete all joinery on the square post before tapering it.

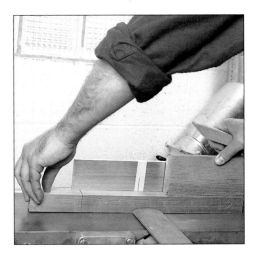

4 **Lower and cut** Once you've got the marks aligned, slowly lower the post onto the knives. As soon as it makes contact, start pushing the post forward. If you hesitate here, you'll likely get a burn mark—especially if you're working with cherry. I'd suggest that you try this a number of times with the power off to get the feel of sliding the guard out of the way as you lower the post. Also, make sure to use a push block *as shown here* to protect your fingers.

5 **Rotate** After you've made a complete pass on one side of the post, lift it up and rotate it one-quarter turn. Then align the two reference marks, lower the post, and make the next cut. Continue like this until you've done all four sides. Stop and check the taper.

Continue to take passes (making sure to taper all four sides) until you're very close to the desired taper. Then adjust the jointer for a very light cut and make a full-length pass without lowering the piece—this should remove any "dish" left by the knives.

JOINTER:
CHAMFERS

Chamfers on the Jointer There are two methods of cutting chamfers on the jointer. The first method, *shown here,* uses a pair of beveled wood strips attached to the jointer bed to guide the workpiece over the cutterhead.

A less accurate way to do this is to tilt the fence to 45 degrees and press the workpiece against the fence to make the cut. The problem with this method is that it's difficult to prevent the workpiece from sliding around as you cut the chamfer.

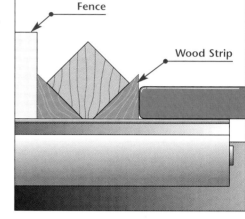
Fence

Wood Strip

1 Attach strips to bed To accurately cut chamfers on the jointer, start by making a pair of 45-degree strips from scrap wood. It's best that they be roughly the same length as your jointer bed. The easiest way to attach the strips to the jointer is with double-sided carpet tape. Attach one strip so that it butts up against the fence, and then position the remaining strip away from the first strip the desired width of the chamfer (*see the drawing at right*).

2 Make the cut Now that you've positioned the strips, all that's left is to cut the chamfer. Position the workpiece in the trough formed by the strips, and push it past the cutterhead. Rotate the piece as desired to cut chamfers on the other corners of the workpiece. This type of setup lends itself well to production runs. It's a lot quieter and faster than cutting the chamfers with a router—and you'll end up with a smoother cut.

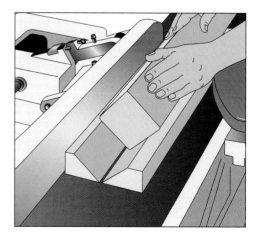

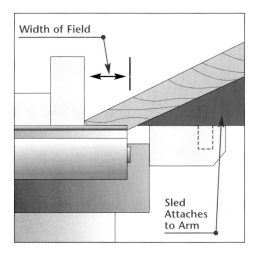

Width of Field

Sled Attaches to Arm

How It Works It's possible to make raised panels on a jointer, as long as it has rabbeting capabilities (*see page 47 for more on this*). The method described here cuts surprisingly smooth panels, as long as your knives are sharp and you take light passes. The secret to making this work is a simple shop-made sled; *see the drawing at left.* The sled holds the panel up at the desired angle to guide it past the cutterhead.

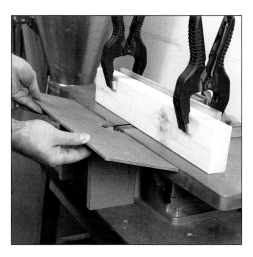

1 Attach sled The sled you make will depend on your jointer. Basically all you need is a pair of angled supports that hold a table (in this case, ¼" hardboard) at the desired angle. Depending on your jointer, you may or may not need to cut a notch near the knives for the sled to butt firmly up against the side of the jointer. Adding a cleat to the base of the supports will allow you to clamp the sled to the jointer stand. (The sled *shown here* is attached to the jointer table with screws.)

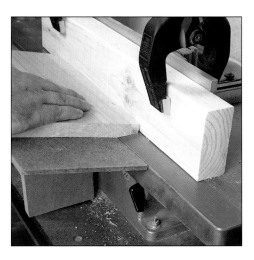

2 Make light cuts Once you've got the sled in place, adjust the infeed table for a light cut. Then adjust the fence over (you may need to clamp an auxiliary fence to it, *as shown here*) to set the width of the field. Then begin by cutting the raised fields on the end grain first. Any chip-out that occurs here will be removed when you joint the fields with the grain. Continue making passes until the jointer stops cutting—since the shoulder will ride on the infeed table when the proper depth is reached, the knives will stop cutting automatically.

Jointers and Planers

JOINTER:
BEVEL CUTS

Tilted Fence In addition to rabbets and chamfers, jointers also excel at cutting smooth bevels. All it takes is an accurately adjusted fence and a smooth, firm grip (*see the drawing at right*). Note: For added accuracy, follow the tip in the sidebar *below*. In order to cut a bevel on a jointer, you'll need to first lay out the intended angle on the workpiece with a sliding bevel or set a sliding bevel with a protractor.

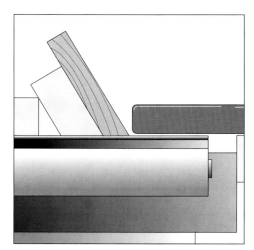

Adjustments To adjust the jointer's fence, loosen the fence clamp to friction-tight and then tilt the fence to the desired angle (*see the drawing at right*). To get a precise angle, place a sliding bevel set to the desired angle on the jointer bed. Position the handle on the bed and the blade on the fence, and tilt the fence until there's no gap between it and the blade. Then press the workpiece firmly against the fence to make the cut.

ACCURATE BEVELS

Whenever you tilt the fence on a jointer, the inclined plane of the fence and gravity tend to work against you—the workpiece wants to slide down away from the fence, resulting in a wavy bevel. Here's a simple trick to avoid this. Just clamp a strip of wood close to the fence so its distance from the fence matches the thickness of the workpiece. This creates a stop, which prevents the workpiece from sliding down. You can also attach the strip to the jointer's bed with double-sided tape (*as shown here*).

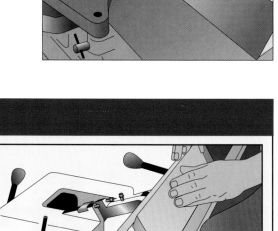

Occasionally you may need to cut a slight taper along the length or width of a post, leg, or other project part. What many woodworkers don't know is that the planer can handle this task nicely with the addition of a simple shop-made sled (*see the sections below*). The advantage that a planer offers is that you end up with accurately thicknessed parts with smooth faces—a combination that no other single stationary tool offers.

Since the sled you make will be good only for tapering a specific part, it makes sense to go to the trouble of making a jig like this only if you're making multiple parts—say, for example, for a set of dining room chairs. If you need only one or two tapered parts, consider tapering them on the jointer (*see pages 48–49 for more on this*).

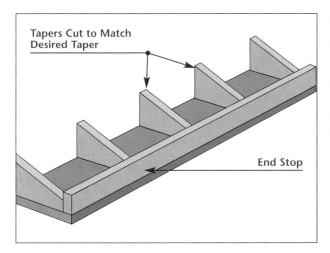

Side Taper Sled The simple sled *shown here* is designed for tapering pieces from side to side. It consists of a plywood base and a series of wedge-shaped supports cut to match the desired taper angle. Screw the supports to the base and then add a stop to the lower end. The end stop holds the workpiece in position—the feed rollers will have a tendency to push the workpiece downhill.

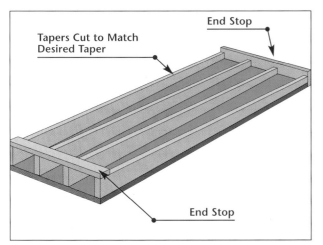

Long Taper Sled The sled *shown here* is for tapering long boards. The difference here is that the angled wedges run the length of the board. Again, it's important to add stops to both ends of the sled to prevent the feed rollers from shifting the workpiece. You'll have the best luck if you feed the sled through the planer with the low end in first.

Jointers and Planers

PLANER:
THIN OR SHORT STOCK

For some time now, there's been a fairly heated debate concerning the safety of planing thin stock. On one side, manufacturers claim that planing thin stock is hazardous, and they all list the minimum thickness you can safely plane on their planers—often ½". On the other side are woodworkers, who often need thinner stock—many projects call for ⅜", ¼", and sometimes ⅛" wood.

Although most manufacturers have built-in stops that limit how close the cutterhead can come to the planer's bed, woodworkers have historically gotten around this by using an auxiliary platform that allows the cutterhead to be closer to the workpiece. Be warned that thin wood can and will explode in the planer with this method. If you choose to try this, make sure that you don't stand directly behind or in front of the planer. Wear safety glasses, take very light cuts, and make sure that your knives are sharp.

Taping to Sled One of the most common ways to plane thin stock is to attach it to a simple sled (a piece of plywood or MDF—medium-density fiberboard) with double-sided tape; *see the sidebar on the opposite page.* For best results, you should apply tape over the full length of the workpiece. If you don't, the rollers and cutterhead can flex the piece, resulting in an uneven thickness.

ShopTip: To remove the thin, fragile stock once it has been planed, drizzle lacquer thinner between the stock and the sled—it'll dissolve the adhesive, and the stock will peel right off.

Feeding Through To adjust the depth of cut, I again recommend that you insert the sled/stock into the planer with the power off and lower the head until it just makes contact with the stock. Then back the cutterhead off a quarter-turn, remove the sled, and begin planing. Although I always suggest that you take light cuts, it's really important here—especially with highly figured woods that tend to shatter when planed too thin. You'll have best luck with cuts less than ¹⁄₁₆", preferably ¹⁄₃₂" to ¹⁄₆₄".

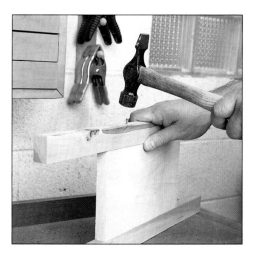

Short Stock Somewhere in the numerous warnings in your planer's manual is a note about minimum length of stock that can be safely planed. Make a note of this, and be sure to follow the manufacturer's recommendations. There is a way you can plane shorter stock: Just temporarily attach a pair of runners to the sides of the stock to be planed, *as shown here.* Just make sure that the runners are thicker than the stock. This way they'll span the space between the feed rollers, allowing the stock to go safely past the cutterhead.

PLANER SLEDS

There are two common ways to plane thin stock on a planer: a sled that hooks onto the planer's bed (*below right*) and a sled that you feed through the planer (*below left*). The advantage of a hook-on sled is that you can plane multiple pieces easily. The disadvantage to this is that a hook-on sled does not support the stock to be planed as well as a feed-through sled when the workpiece is taped directly to the sled.

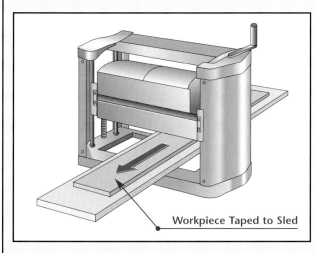

Workpiece Taped to Sled

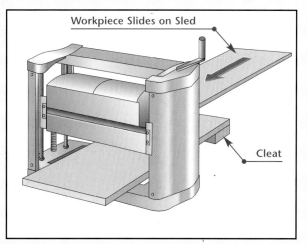

Workpiece Slides on Sled

Cleat

Feed-Though Sled: With this type of sled, the stock is attached to the sled with double-sided carpet tape and the sled/stock is fed through the planer.

Hook-On Sled: A hook-on sled has a cleat on the front edge that hooks onto the bed of the planer. The stock slides on the sled through the planer.

PLANER:
MOLDING

1 Attach auxiliary bed The first step in using most any planer/molder is to attach an auxiliary bed to the bed of the planer. This does a couple of things. First, since some molding knives cut a full profile to clean up the sides of the molding—and therefore would cut into the planer bed—an auxiliary bed is necessary to prevent damage to the knives and bed. Second, an auxiliary bed provides additional clamping space for adding guide rails (*see Step 4 on the opposite page*).

2 Change speed The next step on most planer/molders is to change the feed speed. Some units have a speed lever that you can adjust. Others, like the one *shown here,* require you to swap gears, pulleys, or belts to change speed. Slower feed rates are generally used for the molding operation to provide an improved surface finish. Note: Some manufacturers suggest that you adjust the feed roller pressure when working with wider molding; see your owner's manual. Adjusting the feed rollers ensures that the stock will be securely gripped while you're planing.

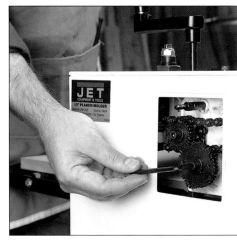

3 Install cutters With the auxiliary bed in place and the speed correct, you can insert the desired molding cutters. Some planer/molders require that you remove the planer blades to do this; on other models, like the one *shown here,* you can leave the knives in place for molding cutters 2" and less in width (for wider cutters, the planer knives must be completely removed). Remove the dust hood to expose the knives, and use the supplied wrench to loosen the lock bars. Remove the spacer and insert the desired cutter; repeat for the remaining cutters.

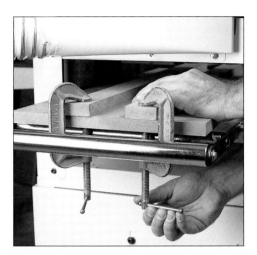

4 **Attach guide rails** Once you've got the cutters installed, you can reassemble the dust hood and hook it up to your collection system. Next, to align and guide the stock so that it passes under the cutterhead at the appropriate point, clamp guide rails to the auxiliary bed *as shown.* Follow the manufacturer's directions on positioning the guide rails, and clamp them securely to the auxiliary bed.

5 **Make the cut** Now you're ready to make some molding. Before you do this, it's always a good idea to run the planer for a couple of minutes to make sure the lock bars that hold the knives/cutters in place are secure. Stop the planer, remove the dust hood, and check and retighten the lock bars. Then read and follow the manufacturer's directions regarding maximum depth of cut. You'll also have best results if you pre-thickness the stock to within $\frac{1}{16}$" of the final thickness. And remember, light cuts will create a smoother finish.

MOLDING CUTTERS

There are a staggering variety of molding cutters available—everything from wide crown molding to tiny beads or even tongue-and-groove cutters to make your own flooring; *see the photo at right.*

Most manufacturers recommend using only their cutters, since they were designed specifically for their machine. Good advice. Also, most planer/molders use a set of three cutters. Steer away from companies that offer single cutters and two counterweights: These can cause severe vibration and can damage your machine.

SHOP-MADE JIGS AND FIXTURES

Unlike many of the other stationary power tools, there aren't dozens of fancy jigs and fixtures that you can make for your jointer and planer. These tools, after all, are task-specific and don't lend themselves to complicated or fancy accessories.

So it may come as a surprise to you, then, to discover that I've devoted a substantial portion of this book to building jigs and fixtures for the jointer and planer. Although there are only seven projects here, they all serve to make your jointer or planer easier and safer to use, as well as add precision and even prevent common problems such as snipe.

In this chapter, I'll start by showing you how to make a dust port for your jointer (*opposite page*). Both the jointer and the planer produce copious amounts of dust and chips—removing these efficiently not only prevents inaccurate cuts due to chip buildup, it also keeps this stuff out of your lungs.

Next, I've included plans for the same push block that I've used in my shop for years (*page 62*). A simple wooden push block like this can save your fingers and help create more-accurate cuts.

The foundation of any jointer is its stand—if it's lightweight and flimsy, it'll vibrate and cause various problems, including rippled or ribbed cuts. To prevent this, you need a stand that's both well constructed and heavy. I've included plans for a shop-made stand that's both of these (*pages 64–67*).

Then it's on to the planer. I'll start with a dust port (*pages 68–71*). Here again, efficient chip conveyance is necessary to keep both the feed rollers and your lungs clean. And just as with the jointer, a planer needs a stout stand that offers solid workpiece support; *see pages 72–75* for plans for a shop-made stand.

Finally, there are two projects that can be used with either tool: a mobile parts cart to hold and transport stock from one machine to the other (*pages 76–79*) and a roller stand that offers much-needed support for long or heavy stock (*pages 80–83*).

Note: Most of the projects described here are designed to fit a specific tool—you'll likely need to alter the dimensions a bit to fit your jointer or planer.

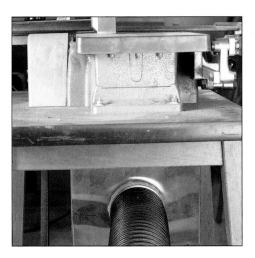

Covering Chute to Collect Dust I've rarely come across a jointer that didn't have some kind of chip chute below the bed to direct chips away from the knives. This helps to make dust collection easy, since all you have to do is cover the chute and add a port. The type of cover you build will depend on the jointer. The one *shown in the photo at left* is made to fit over a wooden chute.

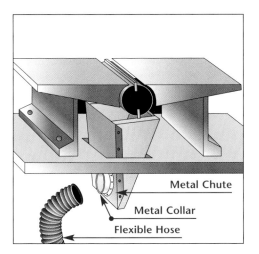

Metal Chute

Metal Collar

Flexible Hose

Exploded View If your chip chute is exposed like the one *shown in the Exploded View at left,* it's best to make the dust port entirely out of sheet metal and then bend lips around the chute *as shown* to achieve the best seal. On my dust port, I even wrapped the sheet metal around the bottom of the chute. Depending on the chute, you may want to go with a combination of wood and sheet metal—wood for the sides and sheet metal for the front.

1 Transfer template to sheet metal The first step in making a dust port for your jointer is to make a paper template. It's a lot easier to mock-up a port with this than it is with sheet metal. Cut an oversized piece, and use some trial and error to find the best place or places to fold it to fit around the chute. When you're happy with the fit (and appearance), transfer the paper template to a piece of sheet metal with a marking pen, *as shown.*

Jointers and Planers

2 Cut the metal Now you can cut out the dust port with a pair of metal snips. Make sure that you wear leather gloves for this to protect your hands from those tiny, annoying metal slivers. The only real challenge here is cutting the hole in the sheet metal for the metal collar that hooks up to your collector via a flexible hose. Your best bet is to drill a series of holes and then slowly enlarge the opening with metal snips until the correct size hole is formed.

3 Attach the metal collar Once you've cut the metal to size, check to make sure that the metal collar fits in the hole. Metal collars like the one *shown here* are available at most home centers in the heating/ventilation aisle. This type of collar has a set of metal tabs that slip into the hole until a stop or metal ring near their base contacts the sheet metal. Then you bend the tabs over to secure the collar. To get the best seal, it's a good idea to apply a bead of silicone caulk around the lip of the hole before installing the collar.

4 Attach to jointer For a wood chute, drill pilot holes in the chute to match those in the lip of the dust port and attach it to the chute with wood screws *as shown.* When attaching the pick-up to cover a metal chute or to cover the opening on an enclosed base, drill smaller pilot holes and use sheet-metal screws. Apply a bead of silicone caulk around the outer edges of the dust port to ensure a good seal.

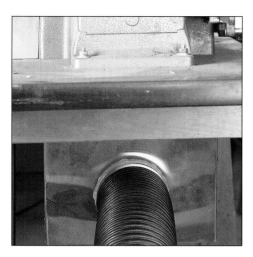

5 **Hook it up** Slip a hose clamp over a flexible hose and secure it to the collar on the pick-up. If possible, run metal pipe to this pick-up instead of flexible hose, since a jointer generates a lot of chips and the metal pipe will convey the chips more efficiently than flexible hose.

Note: A word of warning about this style of pick-up: You need to use it whenever you use the jointer—if you don't, it will quickly jam up and clog with shavings. Resist the temptation to quickly joint an edge without turning on your system and opening the blast gate.

HOOD FOR A CLOSED STAND

Hooking up a dust port to a jointer with a closed stand is simplicity itself. All you need do is cover the dust chute opening with a piece of wood or metal with a collar in it (*see the drawing and photo below*). A piece of ¼" hardboard works well for this. Use a circle cutter to cut a hole to match the collar you're using. Then apply a bead of silicone caulk to the lip of the hole and install the collar. Finally, mount the dust port on the jointer and hook it up to flexible hose or metal ductwork.

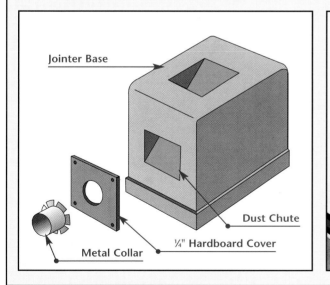

Jointer Base

Dust Chute

¼" Hardboard Cover

Metal Collar

JOINTER:
PUSH BLOCK

A Finger Saver Besides the built-in guard of a jointer, the number-one safety device you can use when jointing wood is a push block. Although there are numerous commercially made push blocks, I've gotten along just fine for years with the shop-made version *shown here.* I prefer an all-wood version like this because if there's a slip and the push block comes in contact with the cutterhead, there's no damage to the knives.

Exploded View The push block *in the drawing* consists of a handle attached to a base that is kerfed at one end to hold a strip of ¼" hardboard. In use, the base presses the workpiece firmly into the bed of the jointer, and the strip of hardboard hooks over the end of the workpiece so that you can safely push it forward. After cutting the handle to shape (*see the pattern below*), I rounded over the edges for a comfortable fit.

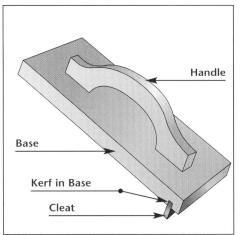

Handle

Base

Kerf in Base

Cleat

HANDLE PATTERN

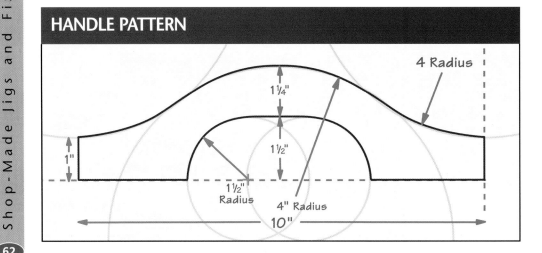

4 Radius

1¼"

1½"

1"

1½"
Radius

4" Radius

10"

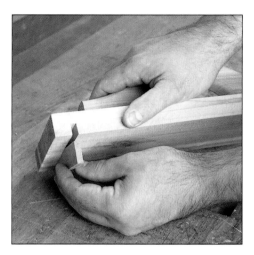

Kerf for Bottom Cleat Cut a kerf in the bottom of the base roughly ⅜" deep and slightly narrower than ¼". If you cut the kerf so it's a bit snug, you can press-fit the hardboard strip in it—when it gets dinged up with use, just pull it out and replace it with a fresh strip. If it's too loose, insert paper shims so that you get a press-fit. If you glue the strip in, you'll have to make a new base when the strip inevitably wears out.

GROUT-FLOAT PUSH BLOCK

Here's another "shop-made" push block that works well in a pinch. If you've ever done any tile work in your house, odds are that you have a grout float lying around somewhere. And a grout float can be pressed into service as a push block; *see the photo below left.*

In most cases, the rubber base of the float will do a fair job of gripping a workpiece. If you notice that it tends to slip, try this trick. Cut a piece of rubber router mat the same size as the float. Then slip it under the float *as shown below right.* You'll be pleasantly surprised to find what a better grip this offers.

Grout Float
A grout float, with its rubber base and sturdy wood handle, works well as a push block in a pinch.

Router Mat
For a better grip, slip a piece of flexible rubber router mat between the base of the float and the workpiece.

JOINTER:
STAND

Heavy and Sturdy There are two things to look for in a jointer stand: weight and sturdiness. The shop-made jointer stand *shown here* offers both. I chose MDF (medium-density fiberboard) for the stand because it weighs in at around 100 pounds per sheet. Since this stand uses up most of a full sheet, its weight helps dampen vibration. A locking rabbet joint is used throughout to create a rock-solid stand.

Note: Although the stand *shown here* is sized for a bench-top jointer, you can alter the dimensions to suit most jointers.

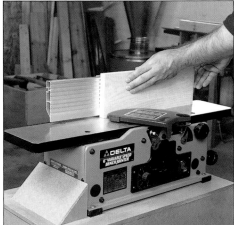

Pullout Bin In addition to being heavy and sturdy, I wanted this jointer stand to be able to handle chips and dust. There are two options here. If you don't have a dust collection system, you can build the pullout bin *shown here.* A hole in the top of the stand, along with a shop-made chute, directs chips and dust into the bin. When the bin fills up, simply slide it out and empty it. If you do have dust collection, don't build the bin. Instead, add a panel in front to fully enclose the base and cut a hole in it for a dust port. Consider adding a baffle inside the stand to direct chips to the port.

1 Create locking rabbet joint The bulk of the jointer stand is constructed with a locking rabbet joint, which consists of a groove in one piece and a tongue (made by cutting a rabbet) on the other piece. The easiest way to cut both parts of the joint is with a dado blade on the table saw. After you've cut the pieces shown in the parts list (*opposite page*), begin by cutting all the ¼"-wide grooves (*as shown here*) and then cut the tongue to fit. As always, you should make test cuts in scrap before moving on to the project parts.

EXPLODED VIEW

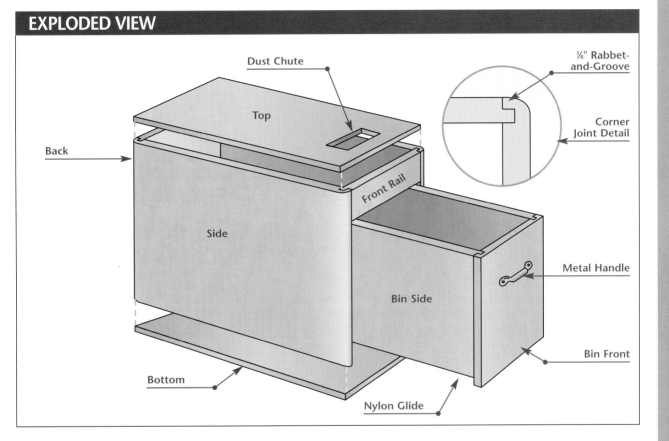

Dust Chute

Top

³⁄₈" Rabbet-and-Groove

Back

Corner Joint Detail

Front Rail

Side

Metal Handle

Bin Side

Bottom

Bin Front

Nylon Glide

JOINTER STAND PARTS LIST

Quantity	Part	Dimensions
2	Stand sides	24" × 26" – ¾" medium-density fiberboard
1	Stand back	13¼" × 24 – ¾" medium-density fiberboard
1	Stand front rail	4" × 13¼" – ¾" medium-density fiberboard
2	Stand top/bottom	14" × 26" – ¾" medium-density fiberboard
2	Bin sides	19³⁄₁₆" × 22½" – ¾" medium-density fiberboard
1	Bin front	12⅜" × 19¹³⁄₁₆" – ¾" medium-density fiberboard
1	Bin back	12⅜" × 19³⁄₁₆" – ¾" medium-density fiberboard
1	Bin bottom	11½" × 22½" – ¼" hardboard
1	Handle	3½" brass pull
4	Nylon glides	1"-diameter

2 Cut dust opening After you've cut the locking rabbet joints, the next step is to make an opening in the top of the stand to direct chips into the bin. Position the jointer on the top and lay out the opening. Then drill a hole for a saber saw blade and cut the opening.

Note: If your jointer has its motor mounted below, you'll need to modify the stand: Cut an opening in the top for the drive belt and add a support below for the motor. Depending on the placement of the motor, it may be impossible to add the pull-out bin; in this case, add a baffle to direct chips to a dust port.

3 Rabbet top and bottom The top and bottom of the stand are rabbeted to fit over the sides and front and back. Here again, the easiest way to cut the rabbets is with a stacked dado blade on the table saw. Make sure to attach an auxiliary fence to your rip fence to prevent damage to the rip fence. Adjust the fence to create a ¾"-wide rabbet, and cut the rabbet on all four edges of the top and bottom *as shown*.

4 Assemble At this point, you're ready to assemble the stand. Before you pull out the glue bottle and brush, it's a good idea to first dry-clamp the parts together to check the fit. If everything looks good, start assembly by applying a bead of glue in the grooves in the sides of the stand. Then spread glue on the matching tongues and press the parts together. Apply clamps to draw the joints tight; *see the photo at right.* When the glue has dried, attach the top and bottom—glue plus a heavy weight are all you need here.

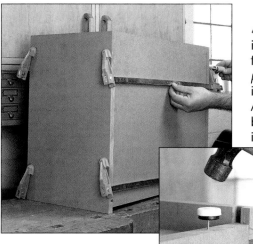

5 Assemble dust bin Once the stand is assembled, you can turn your attention to the pullout bin. Assembly here is similar to the stand's; the big difference is that the front runs the full length and it extends past the bottom of the sides (*see the photo at left*). The extra ¾" creates a lip that conceals and fits into the rabbet on the top inside edge of the stand bottom. After the glue sets, drill pilot holes in the bottom edges of the bin at the four corners for nylon slides that allow the bin to slide in and out smoothly, and tap the slides in place (*inset*).

6 Attach jointer With the stand and pullout bin complete, you can attach the jointer. Position the jointer on top of the stand so that the end aligns with the opening you made in Step 2 for dust and chips. Then mark and drill mounting holes. Attach the jointer to the top with carriage bolts, nuts, and lock washers *as shown in the photo at left.* If your jointer has the motor mounted below, feed the drive belt up through the opening and attach it to the pulley on the jointer.

SHOP-MADE CHUTE

Depending on the location of the dust chute on your jointer, you may or may not need to make a shop-made chute to help direct chips and dust from the jointer into the pullout dust bin. The bench-top jointer *shown here* requires such a chute.

The chute is just a pair of wood wedges connected by a ¼" hardboard top (the top and bottom edges are beveled to match the angle of the wedges). Attach the shop-made chute to the jointer stand with screws from underneath.

Center-Mounted Port Planer pick-ups vary greatly from one machine to another. Most large planers (those over 13") have a custom-designed pick-up that would be hard to duplicate—they're well worth the money.

The pick-up *shown here* is designed for a popular portable planer and can be adapted to fit most small planers under 13". Although you can purchase a pick-up for this style planer, I've had mixed results with them, as most collect chips on one side. I've had much better luck with a shop-made version with a center port, like the one *in the photo at right.*

1 Cut parts The planer pick-up is a tapered box open at one end to fit over the planer cutterhead and tapered on the other end to funnel chips into the dust port (*see the Exploded View on the opposite page*). I went with a mixture of sheet metal and hardwood for a couple reasons. First, I wanted the rigidity that hardwood offers. Second, I needed the thinness and strength that metal offers to fit over the planer knives and to make it easy to add a metal collar to accept a flexible hose. Start by cutting the pieces listed in the parts list *on the opposite page.* Note: You'll likely need to adjust the size of these pieces to fit your planer.

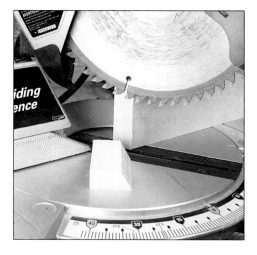

2 Make template The next step in making a dust port for your planer is to create a paper template for the sheet-metal parts. It's a lot easier to mock-up a port with paper than with sheet metal. Cut an oversized piece, and use some trial and error to find the best place or places to fold it to fit around the wood parts. When you're happy with the fit (and appearance), transfer the paper template to a piece of sheet metal with a marking pen, *as shown.*

EXPLODED VIEW

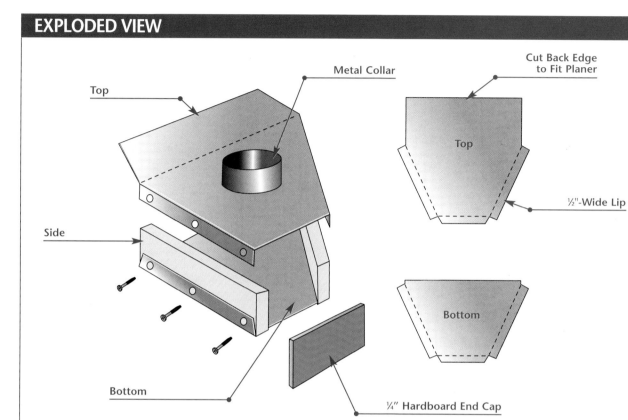

Top

Metal Collar

Cut Back Edge
to Fit Planer

Top

½"-Wide Lip

Side

Bottom

Bottom

¼" Hardboard End Cap

PLANER DUST PORT PARTS LIST

Quantity	Part	Dimensions
2	Sides	3" × 9" – ¾" plywood
1	Top	*12" × 13½" – ¹⁄₁₆" sheet metal or alumininum
1	Bottom	*7" × 13" – ¹⁄₁₆" sheet metal or alumininum
1	End cap	3" × 4½" – ¼" hardboard
1	Collar	4"-, 5"-, or 6"-diameter metal duct collar
		*overall dimensions

3 Cut the sheet-metal pieces Now you can cut out the sheet-metal pieces with a pair of metal snips. Make sure that you wear leather gloves for this to protect your hands from those tiny annoying metal slivers. The only real challenge here is cutting the hole in the sheet metal for the metal collar. Your best bet is to drill a series of holes and then slowly enlarge the opening with metal snips until the correct size hole is formed.

4 Attach the port Once you've cut the metal pieces to size, check to make sure the metal collar fits in the hole. Metal collars like the one *shown here* are available at most home centers in the heating/ventilation aisle. This type of collar has a set of metal tabs that slip into the hole until a stop or metal ring near their base contacts the sheet metal. Then you bend the tabs over to secure the collar. To get the best seal, it's a good idea to apply a bead of silicone caulk around the lip of the hole before installing the collar.

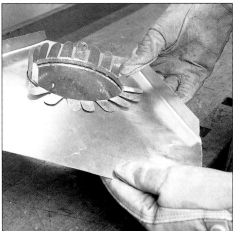

5 Attach to sides Now you can attach the sheet-metal pieces to the wood parts with screws. Your best bet here is to position a metal piece on a wood part and then press an awl through the holes in the metal lips into the wood parts. Drill pilot holes for screws, and then assemble the two pieces. Work on one connection at a time—don't try to assemble the unit as a whole, since it's easy to misalign the parts.

6 **Add the end cap** After you've attached the sheet metal top and bottom to the sides, all that's left is to add an end cap. This is just a piece of ¼" hardboard cut to fit the opening in the rear of the dust port. The ends of the cap are beveled to match the angle of the wood sides. Attach the cap with glue and screws or small brads.

7 **Apply caulk** Since there's a massive quantity of dust and chips to remove when planing, it's imperative that the dust port be as efficient as possible. The best way to guarantee this is to seal the port well with silicone caulk. Apply a generous bead to all seams, paying particularly close attention to the seams between the metal parts, such as the top and the metal collar, *as shown here.*

8 **Hook it up** On my planer, the dust port attaches to a pair of threaded studs that are designed to hold the chip deflector onto the back side of the planer. Remove the nuts that hold the old deflector in place, and drill holes in the sheet metal to match those in the deflector (use the deflector as a template to locate the holes). Then slip the pick-up over the studs and tighten down the nuts. Note: You may find that a strip of self-adhesive foam or rubber weather-stripping applied to the back edge of the bottom will help you get a better seal. Finally, connect a flexible hose (or flexible metal pipe, *as shown here*) from your dust collector to the dust port.

Jointers and Planers

PLANER:
STAND

Support Is the Key Notably the biggest problem with planers is their tendency to snipe the ends of boards. One of the simplest ways to avoid snipe is to fully support the workpiece as it enters and exits the planer. That's what this shop-made planer stand is all about (*see the photo at right*). In addition to this, the stand is built using solid mortise-and-tenon joinery and incorporates heavy materials (the tabletop is made up of a double layer of MDF) to help dampen vibration.

Extension Wings Although all portable and stationary planers come with infeed and outfeed tables or rollers to support a workpiece, they're typically fairly short so that they don't take up valuable shop space. Most often, woodworkers resort to setting up auxiliary support rollers. I've always found this to be a hassle, so I designed this stand with extension wings that flip up when needed and store out of the way when not in use (*see the photo at right*).

Pipe Supports In order for extension wings (like those on the jointer stand *shown here*) to support a workpiece, they must be held firmly in place. The system I've chosen to support the extension wings for this planer stand do just that. The supports are made from pieces of copper pipe and from commonly available fittings. The fittings slip over dowels set into the side of the stand and on a support bar under each table. Note: Make sure to use the thickest-walled copper pipe that you can find, for maximum rigidity.

EXPLODED VIEW

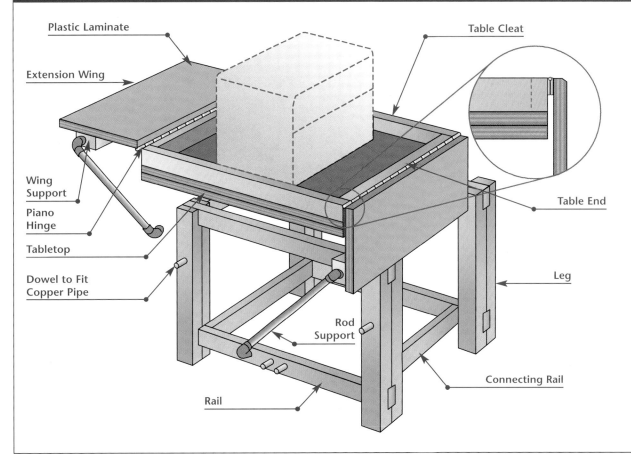

Plastic Laminate

Extension Wing

Wing Support

Piano Hinge

Tabletop

Dowel to Fit Copper Pipe

Rail

Rod Support

Table Cleat

Table End

Leg

Connecting Rail

PLANER STAND PARTS LIST

Quantity	Part	Dimensions
4	Legs	3½" × 3½" – 28" (two pieces of 2×4 for each leg)
4	Leg rails	1½" × 3½" – 30"
4	Connecting rails	1½" × 3½" – 15"
1	Tabletop	21" × 32" – two layers of ¾" medium-density fiberboard
2	Table cleats	2¼" × 30½" – 1½" pine
2	Table ends	2¼" × 21" – ¾" medium-density fiberboard
2	Extension wings	12" × 21" – ¾" medium-density fiberboard
2	Wing laminate	12" × 21" – plastic laminate
2	Wing supports	1½" × 3½" – 21
4	Rod supports	½" copper pipe cut to fit and 90-degree elbows
2	Piano hinges	1½" × 21"

1 Cut mortises As you can see from the Exploded View *on page 73,* each leg of the stand is made up of two lengths of 2×4. Cut the legs to length, and then create the mortises for the connecting rails by cutting matching dadoes and rabbets in each leg piece. When the pieces are glued together, they create a mortise—this is a lot easier than (and virtually as strong as) chopping mortises in solid stock. A stacked dado set in the table saw makes quick work of cutting these (*see the photo at right*).

2 Assemble ends Once the legs have been glued up, cut the side rails to length and assemble two matching ends. Apply glue to the ends of the connecting rails, and drive the parts together with a dead-blow hammer or rubber mallet (*see the photo at right*). Apply a clamp or two over each mortise/tenon joint, and allow the glue to set before moving on to the next step. When dry, plane or sand a slight chamfer on the bottom edges of each leg to prevent splintering when the stand is moved.

3 Connect the ends With the ends of the stand complete, cut the connecting rails to length (*see the parts list on page 73*). Note that all parts are designed for the Makita planer that's *shown here.* You'll need to modify dimensions to fit your planer.

Position the rails so they butt up against the legs *as shown in the Exploded View.* Attach the connecting rails to both the side rails and the legs with glue and screws (*see the photo at right*).

4 **Make the table** Now that the base is complete, you can turn your attention to the table and extension wings. The tabletop is made up of two layers of MDF (medium-density fiberboard), glued together with contact cement. Two sets of cleats form a lip around the top (*see the Exploded View on page 73*). After you've glued the top pieces together, cut the cleats to match the top, and screw them to each other and to the top (*see the photo at left*).

5 **Assemble** After the top is complete, it can be attached to the base. Set the top on the base and position it so it's centered on the base front side-to-side and from front to back. Then clamp it in place temporarily and drill pilot screws through the top and into the connecting rails of the base. Attach the top to the base with 2½"-long wood screws (*see the photo at left*).

6 **Add extension wings** All that's left is to make and attach the extension wings to the table. They're just pieces of MDF, covered with laminate so that the workpiece will slide easily over them. A support bar is glued and screwed under each wing to prevent it from bowing under the weight of the workpiece and to allow for attaching the rod supports.

The wings are attached to the top cleats with piano hinges so that they're flush with the planer's bed (*see the photo at left*). With the wings in the up position, cut copper pipe to span between the wings and the legs. Attach fittings with epoxy (or solder) and add the dowels.

PARTS CART

Mobile Storage

If there's one thing that every woodworking shop has in common, it's that there's never enough horizontal storage space. One of the biggest challenges in preparing wood for a project is finding someplace to set the parts down as you're surfacing them. A parts cart, like the one *shown here,* is the answer. It provides plenty of space to hold parts, including built-in shelves; and it's mobile so that you can wheel it around from the lumber rack to the jointer and planer and then to the bench or table saw.

If you modify its height to match the height of one or more of your stationary power tools, it can even serve as an infeed or outfeed support, since all four of the wheels can be locked to solidly hold the stand in place. The top is covered with plastic laminate not only to protect it from heavy use, but also to create a slick surface for sliding parts on and off. Covering the top with laminate makes the cart useful as a small assembly table as well, since glue can be easily scraped off.

1 Make half-laps The side assemblies of the parts cart are joined together with half-laps. Start by cutting the pieces of the cart to length (*see the parts list on the opposite page*). A table saw fitted with a stacked dado set is the quickest way to cut the half-laps. Set the rip fence as a stop, and use the miter gauge to guide the workpiece into the dado blade. After defining the shoulder, slide the workpiece over and remove the remaining waste. As usual, make test cuts on scraps first before cutting the actual parts.

EXPLODED VIEW

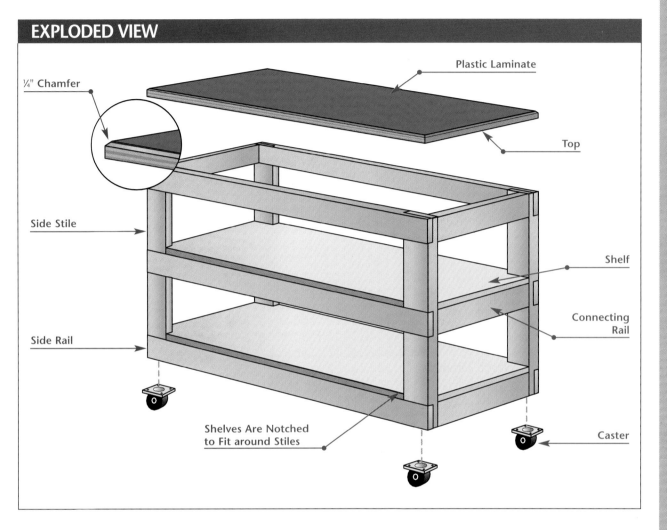

¼" Chamfer

Plastic Laminate

Top

Side Stile

Shelf

Connecting Rail

Side Rail

Shelves Are Notched to Fit around Stiles

Caster

CART PARTS LIST

Quantity	Part	Dimensions
4	Side stiles	1½" × 3½" – 30"
6	Side rails	1½" × 3½" – 36"
6	Connecting rails	1½" × 3½" – 19"
3	Shelves/top	22" × 36" – ½" or ¾" plywood
1	Top laminate	22" × 36" – plastic laminate
4	Casters	2"-diameter swivel with locking mechanisms

2 Build the frames After you've cut the half-laps on the ends of all the side pieces, you can assemble the sides. Start by dry-clamping each side unit to make sure everything fits. If it does, remove the clamps and spread glue on the mating surfaces of the joints. Then assemble the pieces into a unit and apply clamps to each of the half-lap joints. Use a scrap under the clamp (*as shown*) both to spread the pressure equally over the joint and to protect the surface of the wood.

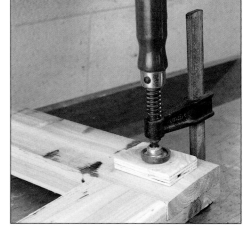

3 Connect the sides Now you can cut the rails to length and assemble the cart; *see the photo at right and the Exploded View on page 77.* **ShopTip**: Since you'll be screwing into the end grain of the rails, use the old cabinetmaker's dowel trick: Drill a ¾" hole an inch in from the bottom edge of each rail end, then spread glue on a short length of ¾" dowel and drive it into the hole. The long grain of the dowel will provide a solid grip for the assembly screws.

4 Add shelves and top After you've assembled the cart, you can add the shelves. Measure the actual dimensions of the cart, and cut two shelves and a top from ½" or ¾" plywood. Lay out and cut notches on the four corners of the shelves to fit around the sides. To install the shelves, you'll need to temporarily remove the screws from one side unit so that you can slip the shelves in place (*see the photo at right*). Attach the top with screws, taking care to set them back an inch from the edge since you'll be chamfering this edge in Step 6.

5 **Laminate the top** With the top in place, the next step is to cover it with plastic laminate. Measure the top and cut a piece of plastic laminate slightly oversized (add 1 or 2 inches to each dimension). Then apply a generous coat (or two) of contact cement to the top and to the laminate. After the cement has set up (follow the directions on the can), place some dowels or strips of wood on the top, set the laminate on top, and remove one strip at a time while pressing it down with a roller (*see the photo at left*).

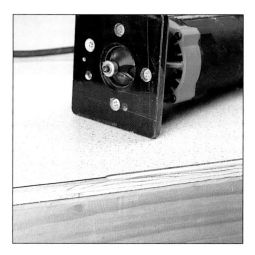

6 **Chamfer the edge** After you've pressed the laminate firmly into the top with a roller—go over it a couple of times to make sure the bond is strong—you can chamfer the edge. Chamfering the edge helps prevent a workpiece from catching on the edge, and it also softens the edge to prevent dings to your lumber. Insert a chamfering bit in a router (or in a laminate trimmer, *as shown*) and rout a ¼" chamfer on all four edges of the top.

7 **Attach wheels** All that's left to complete the parts cart is to add wheels to make it mobile. Although locking wheels cost a bit more, you'll find that they're well worth it when you need to lock the cart in place. Attach the wheels to the bottom of the cart about 6" in from the ends. Use 1" to 1½" wood screws to secure them firmly to the cart (*see the photo at left*).

ROLLER STAND

Support Where You Need It Even long-bed jointers and planers with wide infeed and outfeed tables or rollers need help when you're working with really long or heavy stock. That's where a roller stand comes in. Yes, you can buy metal versions of these, but quality units are expensive and typically have only one roller. The shop-made roller stand *shown here* offers better support with its four rollers, its height is adjustable, and you can build one for less than ten bucks (assuming that you have scrap lumber lying around).

1 Cut grooves in sides To allow you to adjust the height of the roller stand to match your jointer or planer, the legs are made of two pieces held together with splines. The splines fit in ¼"-wide, ⁵⁄₁₆"-deep grooves cut into the leg pieces. Begin by cutting the leg pieces to length (*see the parts list on the opposite page*). Then set up your table saw with a dado set and position the rip fence 1" away from the blade. Make a pass on a leg, flip it end for end, and cut a matching groove on the opposite side. Do this for all four leg pieces.

2 Cut splines in sides The next step is to cut splines to fit the grooves and glue them in place. The splines are just lengths of ¼" hardboard cut to a width of 1⅛". You'll need to cut only four strips—two for each lower leg piece. Once you've cut them to size, glue pairs of strips into the lower leg piece (*see the photo at right*). To make it easy for the upper leg pieces to slide up and down easily on the splines, sand a slight chamfer on the exposed edges of the splines.

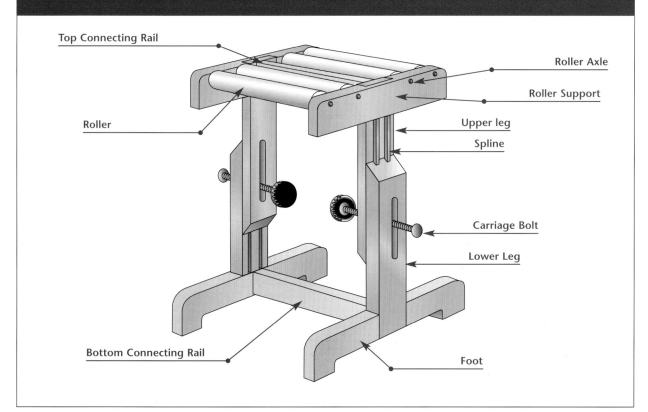

Top Connecting Rail

Roller Axle

Roller Support

Roller

Upper leg

Spline

Carriage Bolt

Lower Leg

Bottom Connecting Rail

Foot

ROLLER STAND PARTS LIST

Quantity	Part	Dimensions
4	Upper/lower legs	1½" × 5½" – 22"
2	Feet	1½" × 3½" – 22"
2	Roller supports	1½" × 3½" – 14"
1	Top connecting rail	1½" × 3½" – 15"
1	Bottom connecting rail	1½" × 3½" – 13"
4	Splines	1⅛" × 18½" – ¼" hardboard
4	Rollers	2" PVC, 12"-long
4	Roller axles	15⅝"-long, ⁵⁄₁₆" rod with metal caps
8	Roller centers	2"-diameter toy wheels
2	Carriage bolts	3½"-long, ⁵⁄₁₆"-diameter
2	Threaded knobs	⁵⁄₁₆" threads

3 Create half-lap joints One end of each leg piece is joined to either a foot or a roller support with a half-lap joint (*see the Exploded View on page 81*). Fit your table saw with a stacked dado set, and cut the half-lap joints in all of the leg pieces as well as the feet and roller supports. Consult the Exploded View frequently because it's important which side of these pieces you cut the half-lap on.

4 Assemble the sides After all the half-lap joints are cut, dry-assemble each of the units—the lower leg and foot, and the upper leg and roller support—to check the fit. If everything looks good, apply glue to the mating surfaces and assemble with clamps. Here again, slip scraps of wood between the clamps and the workpiece to spread clamping pressure and to protect the workpiece (*see the photo at right*).

5 Connect with rails Now that the leg units are glued up, you can assemble them and then connect the two halves with rails. Each side's upper and lower leg pieces are held together with a carriage bolt and a threaded knob. Slots are cut in the upper leg piece to allow it to slide up and down over the bolt. Make the slot by drilling a series of holes and then cleaning out the waste with a chisel. Assemble the legs, cut the rails to length, and assemble the stand with screws (*see the photo at right*).

6 **Add rollers** All that's left to complete the roller stand is to add the rollers. The rollers are made from short lengths of PVC and toy wheels (*see the sidebar below*). The roller axles are just lengths of $\frac{5}{16}$" metal rod. Measure the distance from one edge of the roller support to the other, add $\frac{3}{4}$" for the push caps, and cut four pieces to this length. Space the holes for the rods so the rollers will stand proud of the support. Press an end cap onto a rod; feed it through a support, the roller, and the other support; and press on another cap.

SHOP-MADE ROLLERS

You can make your own rollers with some scraps of PVC and some pre-made toy wheels (or you can make your own wheels with a circle cutter); *see the photo below left*. If you use 2" PVC, you'll find that 2"-diameter toy wheels will fit nicely inside.

If the fit is too loose, all you have to do is wrap a few turns of duct or masking tape around the wheel (*see the photo below right*). What you're looking for here is a press-fit, so the wheel slides in without undue pressure yet stays in place when the roller turns.

Make Your Own Rollers All it takes to make your own rollers is some scraps of PVC pipe and some store-bought or homemade wheels.

Tape Shim for Loose Wheels For the rollers to work smoothly, the wheels need to be snug-fit in the pipe. A turn or two of duct tape will remove any slack.

6 REPAIR AND MAINTENANCE

It's ironic that the two tools that can have the largest impact on the precision of your woodworking—the jointer and the planer—are the two tools that are most often ignored in terms of maintenance and repair. The main reason for this reluctance to regularly fine-tune or "tweak" these machines has to do with the widely held perception that they're extremely difficult to adjust. This just isn't true. In most cases, the adjustments are fairly simple to make. Granted, some require a good bit of patience, but the actual procedure isn't complicated.

The reluctance, I fear, comes from the fact that these machines are generally so reliable that they don't need frequent attention. And the longer we go without adjusting them, the more reluctant we are and the longer we wait. Well, it's time to break that cycle.

In this chapter, I'll begin with the jointer. I'll show you how to clean it and what to look for during a routine inspection (*opposite*

page). Then on to the very important table alignment (*pages 86–87*) and how to keep your jointer well lubricated (*page 88*).

Next, there's detailed instructions on how to adjust the knives. I've included a number of methods, ranging from the low-tech stick method to using a dial indicator or a magnetic knife-holding jig (*pages 89–93*). After that, there's information on how to sharpen jointer knives, including using a nifty jig designed by Veritas (*pages 94–96*).

Then on to the planer. I'll begin with cleaning and inspection (*pages 97–98*) and then cover lubrication (*page 99*). There's detailed information on adjusting planer knives, including the new self-adjusting disposable knives (*page 100*), as well as using magnetic knife-holding jigs (*pages 101–102*).

Sharpening planer blades is covered on *page 103,* and there are details on how and when you can adjust feed rollers (*page 104*) and the cutterhead (*pages*

105–106). In case your planer is a portable, I discuss replacing brushes on *page 107.* Finally, there's help for electrical motor problems and information on how to repair and maintain portable power planers on *pages 108–109 and 110–111, respectively.*

Safety Note: Whenever you work on a planer or jointer, always unplug the machine first and exercise extreme caution when working around the knives—these guys are incredibly sharp and will slice through your fingertips, given the chance.

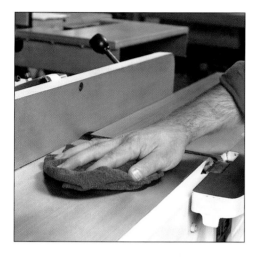

1 Clean the tables In order for a jointer to make a precise cut, the infeed and outfeed tables need to be kept clean and free from debris. Hooking up the jointer to a dust-collection system will help tremendously, but it's still important to wipe down the tables periodically with a clean cloth, *as shown here.* If your tables are protected with wax (*see page 88*), this is all it should take. If not, you may need to wet the cloth with mineral spirits or lacquer thinner to remove any gum or pitch deposits.

2 Check the bed for flatness Many woodworkers think that just because a tool is made from cast iron, it will be perfectly flat and will always stay that way. Not true. Cast iron that's improperly cured can and does warp or twist over time. That's why it's important to periodically check your tables to make sure they're flat.

Lay an accurate straightedge along the length of each bed, and check for gaps with a feeler gauge (*see the photo at left*). Any gaps over 0.010" should be addressed. A reliable machine shop can regrind the surfaces flat, and some tool manufacturers provide this service.

3 Use winding sticks In addition to checking to make sure your tables are flat, you should also check them periodically for twist. The easiest way to do this is with a pair of shop-made "winding sticks" (*see the photo at left*). Place the sticks on one table a couple inches in from each edge. Then sight along the sticks at a low angle to check for twist. If you detect a twist, there are some things to check for (*see pages 86–87*). If these don't cure the twist, the table will need to be reground.

Jointers and Planers

In addition to checking the individual tables for flatness or twist, it's critical to check to make sure that the two tables are level with each other. To do this, first raise the infeed table up to match the height of the outfeed table. Then lay a long, accurate straightedge along both tables and check to see whether they're level. Quite often one of the tables will droop or sag.

Most jointer manufacturers recommend adjusting the gibs to bring a table back into alignment; *see the drawing on the opposite page,* and check your owner's manual for detailed gib-adjustment procedure. In many cases this won't work and you'll have to insert machinist's shims between the table and the base to remove the sag or droop.

Outfeed Table Alignment It's also important that the outfeed table be aligned with the cutterhead. That is, the arc of the cutterhead must align with or be slightly above the plane of the outfeed table. You can check for this with a metal or wood straightedge just as you would when adjusting the knives (*see pages 89–93*). If the outfeed table is either too high or too low, the workpiece will either catch on the table or create snipe at the end of the cut (*see the drawing at right*).

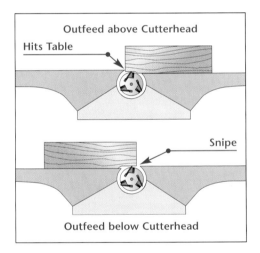

Outfeed above Cutterhead

Hits Table

Snipe

Outfeed below Cutterhead

Adjustable Outfeed Jointers that have adjustable outfeed tables allow you to align the table with the knives without messing with the knives (*see the photo at right*). This is particularly beneficial if you hone the knives in place (*see page 94*)—since if you remove metal with even a light honing, the knives will no longer be level with the table.

On jointers without adjustable outfeed tables, you'd have to adjust each of the knives individually (*pages 89–93*). But if your outfeed table is adjustable, just loosen the locking mechanism and turn the crank to bring the table and knives into alignment.

JOINTER TABLE ANATOMY

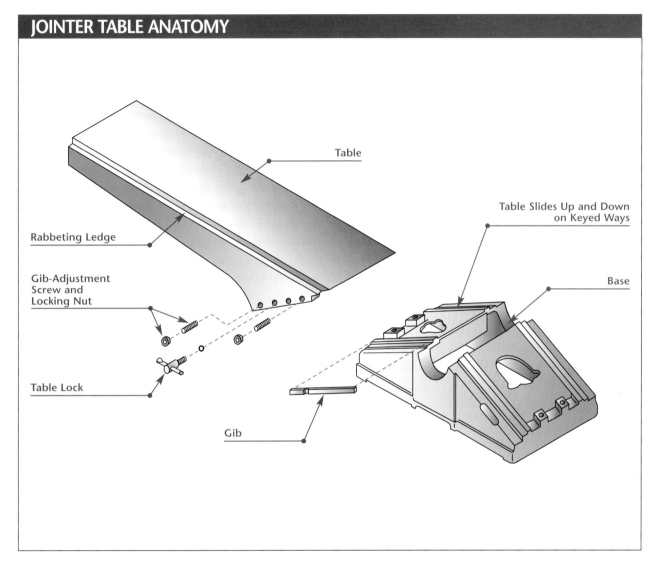

Table

Table Slides Up and Down
on Keyed Ways

Rabbeting Ledge

Base

Gib-Adjustment
Screw and
Locking Nut

Table Lock

Gib

The infeed and outfeed tables of a jointer are attached to the base on inclined planes (called "ways") to allow for adjustment. As you turn the infeed hand wheel, the table slides up and down on the inclined ways to regulate the depth of cut. On most jointers, the ways are dovetail shaped, with the female half on the base and the male half in the underside of the table. The tables are held in place with gib screws and locknuts set into the side of the tables (*see the drawing above*). These screws thread into the gibs, which are flat metal bars located between the mating surfaces of the ways.

1 Wax the tables Call me old-fashioned, but I still prefer to use good old paste wax for my jointer tables. Although there are numerous "hi-tech" spray-ons available, I've always found that paste works just fine. After you've cleaned the tables (*see page 85*), wipe on a light coat of wax *as shown here.* After it has dried to a haze, buff the surface with a clean, dry cloth. This is nice work for a cold or rainy day. It's also a good idea to wax the tables before and after a large project where the jointer gets a lot of use.

2 Oil the pivot points Although most woodworkers do a good job of keeping their jointer's tables clean and lubricated, they often overlook the fence—in particular, the pivot points. That's because not everyone tilts their fence regularly. Without periodic lubrication, the pivot points can rust and seize up. Then when you do want to tilt the fence, you've got a problem. Apply a few drops of light machine oil at least twice a year to the pivot points, and more often if you frequently angle the fence.

3 Grease the sliding parts Unlike the tilting mechanism, the fence itself generally gets adjusted regularly when you slide it back and forth across the width of the jointer to position a workpiece. Not only is the fence constantly adjusted, but the sliding surfaces are exposed to shop dust and grime. That's why it's important to clean off the sliding surfaces regularly and apply a light coat of grease, *as shown here.* I've found that white lithium grease works well for this.

Many woodworkers feel that some form of magic is required to adjust jointer knives accurately. Granted, these can be tricky, but all it really takes is a scrap of wood and a lot of patience. The sequence described here—adjusting the knives with a stick—has been around as long as jointers have been made. It's surprisingly accurate, and the patience is required mainly because of the inherent movement of the knives that occurs when the gibs or locking bars are tightened down.

Typically, when a screw or bolt is fully tightened, it causes the part it's being tightened against to shift or twist. Even a slight movement can throw knife alignment off. And this is where the patience comes in. Adjusting the knives on a jointer is very straight-forward, but it does require a lot of back and forth adjusting—set the knives, check them, loosen and readjust, check them again, readjust…. You get the idea.

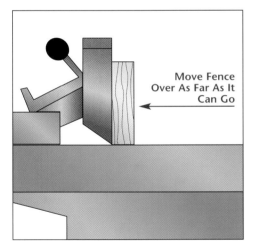

Move Fence
Over As Far As It
Can Go

1 Set the fence To use the stick method for adjusting jointer knives, start by unplugging the machine. Since you'll likely be adjusting the knives because they've been sharpened, take the time to clean the slots and locking bars with mineral spirits. Then insert a knife and locking bar, and tighten the nuts or screws so they're friction-tight—that is, they're held in place but can still be adjusted. Next, slide the jointer fence to one extreme of the table (*see the drawing at left*).

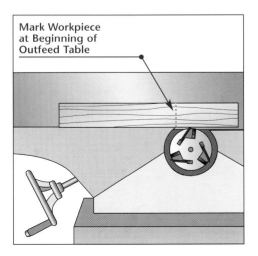

Mark Workpiece
at Beginning of
Outfeed Table

2 Mark a stick Select a scrap of straight wood that's a foot or so long, and place the stick on the outfeed table so that it extends past the cutterhead and over the infeed table (*see the drawing at left*). The make a mark on the stick where it touches the edge or beginning of the outfeed table.

3 **Rotate cutterhead** Now comes the fun part. Rotate the cutterhead forward by hand (don't grab the cutterhead to do this; instead, rotate it by moving the drive belt) so that it lifts the stick and drags it forward slightly. If the knife doesn't touch the stick, adjust it up so it does. What you're looking for here is about ⅛" of movement. This means that the cutterhead is roughly 0.003" above the outfeed table. If it drags the stick more than that, it's too high and needs to be adjusted down.

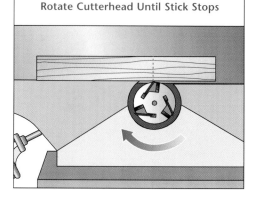

Rotate Cutterhead Until Stick Stops

4 **Make a second mark** Once you've got the knife adjusted so that it lifts and drags the stick about ⅛", make a second mark on the stick where it touches the beginning of the outfeed table (*see the drawing at right*). These two marks then define the arc of the cutterhead at the desired height. If all the knives lift and drag the stick the same distance (on both ends), the knives are in perfect alignment.

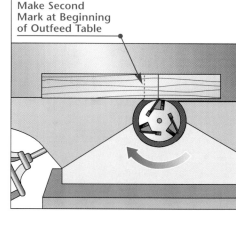

Make Second
Mark at Beginning
of Outfeed Table

5 **Reset fence** After the knife is set on one side, slide the fence over to the other side of the table (*see the drawing at right*). Then place the stick against the fence so that the first mark you made touches the beginning of the outfeed table. Rotate the cutterhead and check to see whether the stick is dragged the same length. Odds are that it won't be and that you'll need to adjust the knife. Use a scrap of wood to force the knife up or down and then recheck. Then tighten the locking bar and recheck the knife with the stick. Adjust, tighten, and recheck and repeat as necessary.

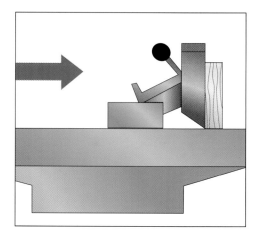

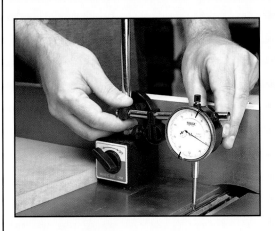

1 Set it up For the utmost in accuracy, you can use a dial indicator like the one *shown here* to adjust your jointer knives. Although dial indicators take a bit of time to set up, you can adjust your knives in thousandths of an inch. I like to clamp a square scrap to the outfeed table *as shown* in order to keep the dial indicator at the same reference point along the table. An optional magnetic base allows you to anchor the indicator firmly in place.

2 Loosen/adjust knives Adjust the position of the indicator so that the knives will be set the height above the table recommended by the manufacturer. With the tip of the indicator resting on the knife at top dead-center, loosen the gib bolts or screws to be friction-tight and then adjust the position of the knife so that the indicator reads the desired setting (*see the photo at left*).

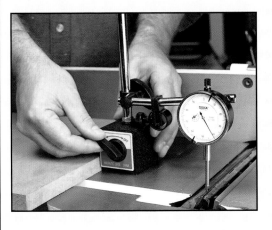

3 Move to other end Release the magnetic base of the dial indicator and slide it along the scrap to the other end of the table (*see the photo at left*). Adjust the knife as you did in Step 2. Slide the indicator back to its original position, check to make sure the knife didn't slip out of position, and adjust if necessary. Continue sliding the indicator back and forth, checking knife height until it's correct. Then tighten the gib screws or bolts, working from the center toward the ends.

Jointers and Planers

1 **Find top dead-center** There are a number of magnetic knife-setting jigs on the market that make adjusting knives less of a chore. They use a set of strong magnets to hold the knife in perfect position while you tighten the locking bolts. To use one of these jigs, you'll need to find where the top of the cutterhead arc is, or top dead-center. Place a scrap of wood on the outfeed table so that it extends over the cutterhead. Rock the cutterhead back and forth until the cutting edge of the knife just barely touches the underside of the scrap, and make a mark on the fence.

2 **Scribe the fence** To save yourself the trouble of locating top dead-center every time you adjust the knives, use a small try square and an awl to scribe or scratch a heavy reference line onto the fence (*see the photo at right*). If necessary, darken the line with a felt-tip marker to help make it easier to see.

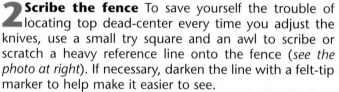

3 **Position jig** With top dead-center clearly marked on the fence, you can position the jig on the jointer. Align the marks on the jig with the line you scribed in the fence (*see the photo at right*). On some jigs, the manufacturer suggests that you make an additional mark on the fence to correspond with a mark on the rear of the jig. This makes aligning the jig even more precise.

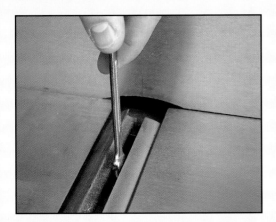

4 **Loosen bolts** To set the knives, lift the jig off the table and loosen the locking bar bolts or screws (*see the photo at left*). Here again, you'll likely be adjusting the knives after they've been sharpened. Before you insert the sharpened knives, clean the cutterhead slots and the locking bars with mineral spirits and wipe them off with a clean, dry cloth.

5 **Adjust the knives** Insert the clean and sharpened knives into the cutterhead slots and insert the locking bars (*see the photo at left*). Tighten the locking bar bolts or screws just friction-tight and reposition the magnetic setting jig, taking care to align it with the marks you made on the fence. Make sure that you don't overtighten the locking bar bolts or screws, or else the magnets in the jig won't be able to lift the knife into the desired position.

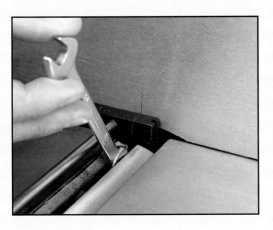

6 **Tighten the locking bars** Once the knife is aligned by the jig, you can begin tightening the locking bar bolts or screws. Tightening sequence varies from one manufacturer to another—the most prevalent has you starting in the center and working out toward the ends. Tighten each bolt just a bit in turn, and continue tightening a little at a time until the locking bar is secure. If you tighten a bolt or screw completely, it can cause the knife to twist out of position. Run the jointer for a few minutes, and then retighten each bolt or screw.

JOINTER:
SHARPENING KNIVES

The knives in your jointer will eventually dull and need to be resharpened. There are two basic ways you can handle this. If the knives are in reasonable shape (no nicks or severely blunted edges), it may be possible to hone them in place with a sharpening stone (*see the jig shown below*). Please note that honing doesn't replace sharpening—it simply lengthens the time required between sharpenings.

To sharpen jointer knives, you'll first need to remove them. Mark each knife and the cutterhead so you can return the knives to their original slots. Most manufacturers suggest that you remove only one knife at a time. If you don't have two sets of knives, consider purchasing some flat bar stock to insert while the knives are being sharpened: Removing all the knives at once has been known to warp the cutterhead.

Honing Jig   There are a couple of honing jigs available for quickly bringing up a fresh edge on your jointer or planer knives. The one *shown here* has two different shaped stones embedded in a wooden holder. The square stone is used to lap the back of the knife, and the other stone is beveled to match the angle of the knives. When using one of these, make sure that the knives are clean and that the machine is unplugged prior to sharpening.

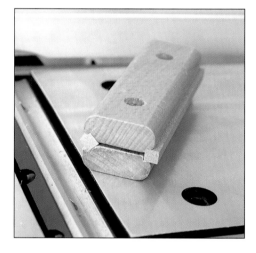

Honing   You can extend the time between knife sharpenings by honing the knives in place. Make certain the knives are completely free from resin or pitch before honing them. Butt the stone of the honing jig up against the knife and push it forward in a long, gentle stroke (*see the photo at right*). Make sure to keep the stone pressed firmly against the knife or else you'll alter the bevel angle. A couple of strokes per knife is all it takes.

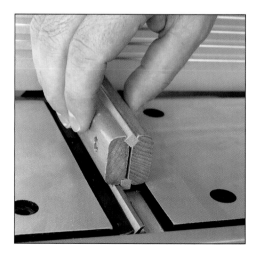

1 Prepare lapping surface To use the Veritas sharpening jig, you'll first need to prepare a lapping or sharpening surface since most oilstones and waterstones are too short to handle the long knives of a jointer. You can make a long lapping surface by attaching silicon-carbide sandpaper to a piece of ¼" tempered glass with spray adhesive (*see the photo at left*). (Replacement louvers for jalousie-style windows work great for this, and their edges are already rounded over for safety.)

2 Lap back of blade To achieve a truly sharp edge, you need to sharpen or hone both halves of the intersecting edge that forms the point. First lap the back of the knife by rubbing it back and forth along the lapping plate (*see the photo at left*). Because most knives will have grinding marks left by the manufacturer, you'll need to remove these; lap the knife until the marks from at least ¹⁄₁₆" back from the leading edge of the knife are gone along its entire length.

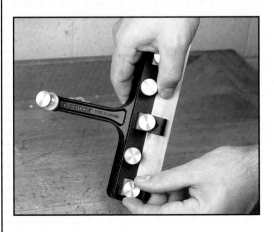

3 Insert knife in jig Once the back has been lapped, you can turn your attention to the bevel. Start by clamping the knife in the sharpening jig, following the manufacturer's directions. Insert the knife under the clamps so that it's parallel with the edge of the jig and overhangs the edge by about ⅛" (*see the photo at left*). Before tightening the clamps, slide them up as far as possible to exert the maximum clamping force.

Jointers and Planers

(continued)

4 Adjust the stops One of the nifty features of the Veritas sharpening jig is the built-in stops. When butted up against the back of the knife, it allows you to accurately position each of the remaining knives without the fuss of aligning them individually. To use these, loosen the thumb nut, slide the stop forward, and tighten (*see the photo at right*). When you change knives, loosen only the clamps and then slide the next knife to be sharpened up against the stops.

5 Adjust the bevel Now that the knife is clamped firmly in place, you can adjust the bevel angle. Place the jig on a flat surface, and loosen the locking nut and turn the adjusting screw to achieve the desired sharpening angle (*see the photo at right*). Tighten the locking nut and then check the setting by taking a few strokes on the lapping plate. If material is being removed from just the heel or the toe of the knife, adjust the screw as necessary.

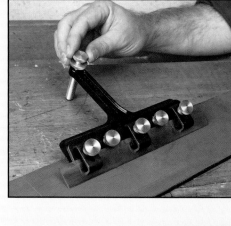

6 Sharpen With everything set, it's time to sharpen the knife. Place the jig on the lapping plate, making sure that the tip of the adjusting screw is on a flat surface (*see the photo at right*). Apply even pressure along the knife and take firm, long strokes. Veritas recommends applying pressure along the push stroke only, to avoid creating a wire edge on the knife. You can also hone a microbevel by turning the adjusting screw a half-turn clockwise and continuing to sharpen.

There's no doubt about it: Regardless of size, most planers get worked hard. For years all I had in my shop was a small 12" portable planer. I've surfaced literally thousands of board feet with that little guy. The secret to its longevity? Regular maintenance. In many cases, all I'm talking about is simply keeping it clean and inspecting it periodically.

Since there are more moving parts in a planer versus a jointer—the feed rollers, cutterhead, and table—they need a bit more attention. Sawdust left in a machine will eventually affect its performance by gumming up gears and feed rollers and even forcing the cutterhead out of alignment.

If you get in the habit of cleaning the planer before you use it—wiping down the posts, blowing out any sawdust—you'll be pleased to find that not only will the planer last longer, it'll cut more precisely, too.

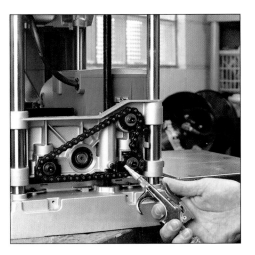

1 Clean the gears Even with good dust collection, sawdust and chips will still manage to weasel their way into the drive gears of the planer. This is to be expected, since a planer is removing such copious amounts of wood. At least a couple of times a year, and before and after a large planing job, I'll remove the cover plates or sides of the planer and clean the gears and rollers with a burst of compressed air. If you don't have compressed air in your shop, use a vacuum and a stiff-bristle brush to pry out the debris.

2 Clean the posts Besides the cutterhead and rollers, the posts of a planer are subject to the most movement because you're constantly changing the depth of cut. No matter whether your cutterhead moves or the table moves, it's important to keep the posts as clean as possible. For the most part, all this takes is wiping them down regularly with a clean, dry cloth, *as shown here.* If you've been planing resinous woods (like pine), it may be necessary to use some mineral spirits or lacquer thinner to remove pitch and gum deposits.

Jointers and Planers

3 Inspect the knives Most planer manufacturers recommend that you regularly inspect the planer knives for wear and tear as well as double-checking that the locking bars are tight—typically after every 50 hours of use. Consult your owner's manual for recommended intervals.

Regardless of the quality of the planer, planing is hard on the machine. There's a lot of inherent vibration, and the locking bar bolts can and do loosen over time. This is one of those preventive maintenance tasks that really can save you from having downtime and expensive repairs.

4 Check the dust port Although the obstruction in the dust port *shown here* is severe—you'd certainly notice that it was plugged, as chips would be flying out around the workpiece—it's a good idea to regularly check your dust port to make sure chips and shavings haven't gotten caught inside. When this happens, efficiency is lost and your dust-collection system can't work to its full potential. This is particularly important to check before beginning a large planing job.

CHECKING THE BED

Just as with the tables of a jointer, the bed of a planer must be flat and true in order to make accurate cuts. It's a good idea to check the bed of your planer periodically to make sure it's flat. To do this, place a known accurate straightedge diagonally across the bed *as shown in the photo at right*. Then check for gaps with a feeler gauge. Any gaps over 0.010" should be repaired. Cast-iron beds can be reground, and sheet metal beds can be hammered flat, at any reliable machine shop.

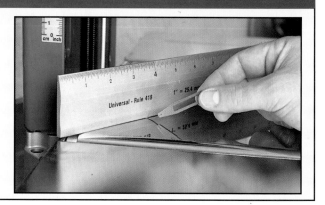

Repair and Maintenance

1 Lubricate the bed Since the beds on most portable planers are sheet metal, I prefer to use a spray-on coating. I've found that these new coatings do a better job of protecting sheet metal over time than paste wax, and they create a really slick surface that reduces workpiece friction. Most of these are sprayed on and then buffed a few minutes later once the coating dries. Even small cast-iron tables (*like the one shown here*) will benefit from this type of coating. As always, lubricate the bed periodically and before and after big planing jobs.

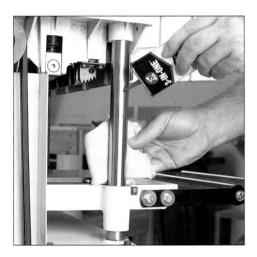

2 Oil the posts In order for the cutterhead or table to move smoothly up and down when you're adjusting depth of cut, you'll need to keep the posts clean (*see page 96*) and well lubricated. A drop or two of light machine oil on each post is all it takes (*see the photo at left*). To prevent sawdust from glomming onto the post and turning into a thick goo, wipe away any excess oil with a clean, dry cloth.

3 Lubricate the gears The gear system within a planer is primarily responsible for turning the infeed and outfeed rollers. Since these gears are in constant use, they will benefit from periodic lubrication (*see the photo at left*). Consult your owner's manual for both the recommended lubricant and the suggested frequency of lubrication. Depending on use, the frequency could vary anywhere from daily to once or twice a year.

SELF-ADJUSTING PLANER KNIVES

I've changed a lot of planer knives over the years, and I've never come across a system that's as quick and easy to use as the self-adjusting system that Makita features in their newest portable planer. From start to finish, they make this often-frustrating job a snap. They've thoughtfully engineered this planer to make changing knives a coffee break job instead of an all-day fiasco: A built-in cutterhead lock, double-sided knives, a long-handled socket wrench (to keep your fingers away from the sharp blades), magnetic holders that both grip and align the knives, and a retaining bracket that automatically locks the blades in the perfect position are just some of the reasons that knife changing on this machine is so easy.

Double-Edged Disposable Knives A Makita planer's knives are held in place by two magnetic holders. They're sharpened on both sides so they can be flipped end for end when one side dulls. When both sides are dull, you discard the narrow knives and replace them with a fresh set.

1 Loosen mounting bolts To change the knives on the Makita planer, start by unplugging the machine and then loosen the thumb screws that hold the chip deflector in place and remove it. Then remove the right side cover and rotate the cutterhead until it automatically locks in position with the mounting bolts facing up. Now you can use the long-handled socket wrench provided to loosen the mounting bolts (*see the photo at right*).

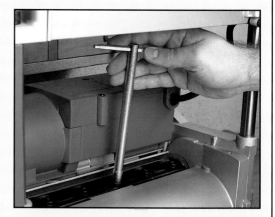

2 Lift out the knife Place the two magnetic holders supplied on the set plate, and push them forward until the small claws on the end contact the knife. Remove the installation bolts, and then grip the magnetic holders and raise them straight up. The knife can now be flipped end for end to expose a fresh edge (or replaced if both sides are dull) and realigned by setting the edges 1mm (3/64") past the plate. Reinstall the magnetic holders, and slip the heel of the set plate into the slot in the cutterhead. Reinstall the mounting bolts—and you're done.

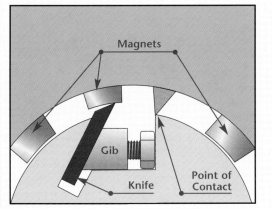

Magnetic setting jigs for the planer work on the same principle as those for the jointer. A set of strong magnets are held in a plastic or metal head that fits the curve of the cutterhead. A third magnet in the jig holds the knife in position while you tighten the gib screws or locking bar bolts. On the jig *shown here,* correct placement is achieved by butting the plastic leg of the jig (the green triangular piece to the right of the knife) up against the edge of the cutterhead.

1 Remove hood The first step in using a magnetic knife-setting jig for the planer is to unplug the planer and remove the dust hood or chip deflector to gain access to the knives (*see the photo at left*). In most cases, the hood or deflector is held on with a pair of thumb screws. **Caution:** The exposed knives are very sharp; exercise extreme care when working around these. It's also a good idea to clear away any dust or chips with a blast of compressed air or with a vacuum.

2 Loosen gib screws Once you've gained access to the knives, the next step is to loosen the gib screws or bolts that press the gib or locking bar into the knives to hold them in place in the cutterhead (*see the photo at left*). Note: If your planer uses elevating screws to adjust the height of the knives, back these off so that they don't interfere with the operation of the magnetic jig; consult your owner's manual for more on this.

Jointers and Planers

(continued)

3 Remove the knife With the gib bolts or screws loose, you should be able to lift out the gib (or locking bar, as it's sometimes called). Insert the tip of a screwdriver under one of the gib screws or bolts, and pry the gib up—it should come up easily, and if it doesn't, double-check to make sure all the bolts are sufficiently loose. Once the gib is out, carefully lift out the knife (*see the photo at right*).

4 Clean the gib slot Now that the gib and knife are removed from the cutterhead, take the time to clean out the slot. Remove any sawdust or chips with compressed air or a vacuum, and follow this with a clean, dry cloth (*see the photo at right*). If you notice any pitch or resin deposits, dampen the cloth with some lacquer thinner or mineral spirits and scrub the slot clean. Clean the gib and knife as well before re-installing them.

5 Position the knife Insert the gib in the slot, and slip in the knife. Adjust the gib screws or bolts until they just barely hold the knife in place. Position a magnetic jig at each end of the cutterhead, following the manufacturer's directions. Press down on the jig so that the magnets grip the cutterhead and the knife. Tighten the gib bolts or screws in small increments, working from the center of the knife to the edges, until the knife is held securely in place (*see the photo at right*). Repeat for the remaining knives.

Because of their width, I recommend that you have your planer knives sharpened professionally. The only exception to this is if you have a Tormek system and Tormek's jointer/planer knife-sharpening jig (*described on page 31*). This system is quite capable of handling most home-shop planer knives. If you haven't used a local sharpening service in the past, check with your woodworking buddies or the local woodworking club or guild for a recommendation.

I've had mixed results over the years from sharpening services. Although most do a fair job, occasionally you'll run up against one that doesn't. Check to make sure that they've sharpened planer knives before, and be careful to give exact instructions as to desired angle. I had one service grind my knives to the wrong angle because I just assumed they'd duplicate the existing angle. They didn't, and the knives had to be reground. One way to get around all this is to use a planer that accepts disposable knives (*see the sidebar below*).

Power Planer The knives on a portable power planer are much narrower than on a thickness-planer and so can be easily sharpened using standard sharpening techniques. Some manufacturers include a jig to sharpen their knives. The Makita power planer that I own has a nifty jig that holds both knives at the same time. You just insert them in the jig and sharpen (*see the photo at left*). The angle is preset, and you can quickly bring them to a sharp edge in no time.

DISPOSABLE BLADES

One of my favorite improvements to planers in recent years has been the introduction of disposable blades, like the ones *shown in the photo at right*. These double-sided blades can be discarded when both edges have become dull.

Since they're both thinner and narrower than standard blades, they're less expensive. Add to this the fact that you don't have to wait one or two weeks for your blades to get sharpened, and they make a lot of sense.

PLANER:
ADJUSTING ROLLERS

1 Loosen the locknut On some planers, particularly on planer/molders, you can adjust the feed-roller pressure to compensate for different operations and types of wood. To adjust the feed rollers, start by loosening the jamb nuts that lock the rollers in position (*see the photo at right*). Note that on these same posts are nuts that control the spring pressure—these are factory-set and should not be fiddled with.

2 Position the gauge block Next, make a reference gauge block, following the manufacturer's instructions in the owner's manual. Then insert this gauge block under the center of the feed roller and raise the table (or lower the cutterhead) until the roller just barely touches the block (*see the photo at right*). Note: You should be able to slide the block back and forth along the full width of the feed roller.

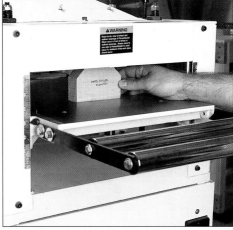

3 Adjust In most cases, you'll have multiple gauge blocks of varying heights designed for specific operations. Adjust the feed rollers by turning the threaded bushings on the posts *as shown in the photo at right.* Then slide the desired gauge block under the feed roller. Here again, it'll be adjusted correctly when you can just barely slide the guide block back and forth along the entire length of the feed roller. Retighten the jamb nuts and recheck; repeat this procedure for the outfeed roller.

Outside of adjusting the knives and feed rollers on a portable planer (*see pages 100–102 and page 104, respectively*), there's not a lot more you can do in terms of adjustment. That's because most portable planers don't have an adjustable pressure bar or chip breaker (*see the drawing below*). It's not that you can't adjust them—they're not there at all. You'll usually find these only on larger planers with knives 15" and wider.

Compare the drawing below with the simplified drawing *on page 15.* Note that there is nothing directly on each side of the cutterhead. Instead, these smaller planers rely on the infeed and outfeed rollers instead of a pressure bar, and they depend on sharp knives to prevent chip-out.

There is one other thing to check for that's always adjustable on larger planers and on some smaller planers: that the cutterhead is parallel to the planer's bed or table (for more on this, *see page 106*).

CUTTERHEAD ANATOMY

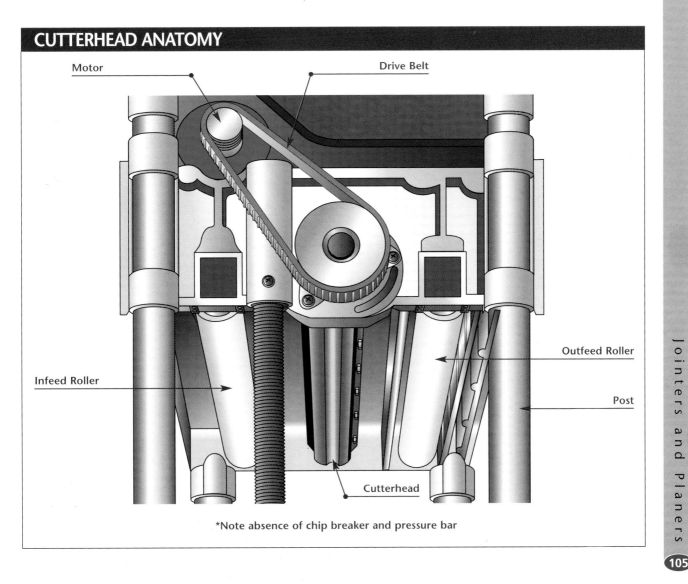

Motor

Drive Belt

Outfeed Roller

Post

Infeed Roller

Cutterhead

*Note absence of chip breaker and pressure bar

1 Access the cutterhead Consult your owner's manual for the recommended procedure for checking and adjusting the cutterhead/bed parallelism. In most cases, the manufacturer suggests that you remove one or both of the side panels of the planer for better access (*see the drawing at right*). On some portable planers, you can get to the adjustments from inside the planer, but note that there's not a lot of knuckle room there.

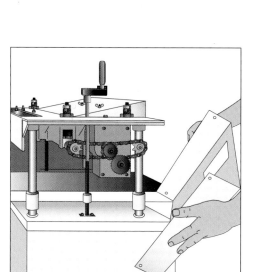

2 Position gauge block Next, make a wooden gauge block out of a scrap of hardwood. Then insert this gauge block under the center of the feed roller and raise the table (or lower the cutterhead) until the roller just barely touches the block (*see the photo at right*). Note: You should be able to slide the block back and forth along the full width of the feed roller. If you can't, the cutterhead or table needs to be aligned.

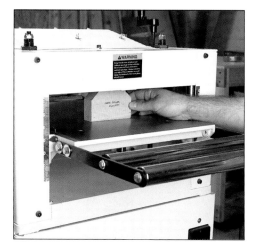

3 Loosen bolts With the side panels removed, you should have complete access to the posts on which the cutterhead or table moves up and down. Typically, there is a set of bevel gears that will allow adjustment of the position of the cutterhead or table. Loosen the jamb nut and adjust the bevel gear until you can slide the gauge block back and forth under the cutterhead. When you can, retighten the jamb nut and check again.

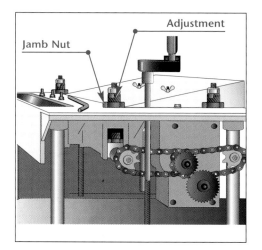

Jamb Nut

Adjustment

The brushes in a portable planer motor provide a way to transfer electrical current to a rotating object (in this case, the armature). Brushes are made up of highly conductive carbon particles pressed together in a small rectangular bar.

One end of the brush is curved to match the diameter of the armature. A spring inserted between an end cap/wire assembly and brush pushes the brush against the armature.

By the very nature of this pressing and rubbing action, the brushes will wear down over time; *see below*. Another thing to check brushes for is spring tension. If there isn't enough pressure, the brushes will make intermittent contact and your planer will operate sluggishly. If in doubt, replace them.

Access Caps The ease with which you can access a planer's brushes depends primarily on the manufacturer. Most manufacturers make this fairly easy to do by providing easily accessible brush caps, like those *shown here* on a Makita planer. Just unscrew the cap and set it aside. If the springs are in good shape, they should force out the metal end of the brush so that you can pull it out. If the springs are bad, you may need to pry out the metal end in order to pull out the brush.

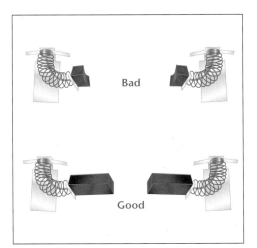

Bad

Good

Worn Brushes OK, so you've removed the brushes—how do you tell a good brush from a bad brush? What you're looking for here is a nice even gloss on the end of the brush. If it's scarred, it needs to be replaced. As to the length, it's difficult to know when to change brushes unless you know how long they were to start with. As a general rule of thumb, if you've got less than ¼" left in length, replace them.

Jointers and Planers

REPLACING A MOTOR

1 Disconnect wires Planer and jointer motors occasionally go bad and need to be repaired or replaced. In both cases, you'll need to remove the motor. Start by removing the access plate on the motor that covers the wires. Before removing any wire nuts, make a rough sketch of the wiring, including wire colors. Then remove one wire nut at a time to free all the wires (*see the photo at right*). Loosen the cord clamp and remove the cord from the motor.

2 Remove mounting bolts The next step is to loosen and remove the bolts that secure the motor to the stand (*see the photo at right*). These may be bolts that thread directly into the stand, or through bolts that are held in place with nuts (*as shown here*). Note: Once the motor is removed, it's a good idea to re-install the bolts in the stand to keep from misplacing them.

3 Remove belt After you've removed the mounting bolts, you'll be able to lift up the motor and slide off the drive belt (*see the photo at right*). This is a good time to inspect the belt for wear and tear and to consider replacing it if worn (*see the sidebar on the opposite page for more on belts*). If the belt is cracked or the edges are frayed, it should be replaced.

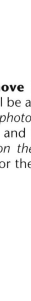

4 Remove pulley if necessary If you're planning on replacing the motor with a new one, you'll need to remove the pulley so that you can install it on the new motor. To do this, loosen the pulley setscrew with an Allen wrench or a screwdriver and remove the pulley (*see the photo at left*). If you're lucky, you may be able to pull it off by hand. If not, try tapping it with a rubber hammer to free it; otherwise you may have to resort to a bearing puller.

V-BELTS: STANDARD AND LINK

There are two basic types of belts that drive jointers or planers: V-belts, and an interlocking style. V-belts come in a variety of thicknesses to fit different sizes of pulleys. They also come in various diameters to span a wide range of distances between pulleys. If you've got a number of belt-driven machines in your shop, consider purchasing a couple feet of interlocking belt (*see the drawing below right*). This style belt uses links that can be interlocked to form any size belt you need—sort of a "universal" belt. Link belts are available from most mail-order woodworking catalogs and some motor repair shops.

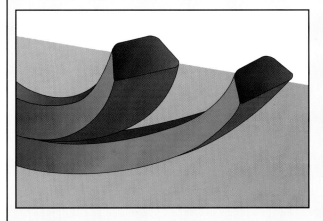

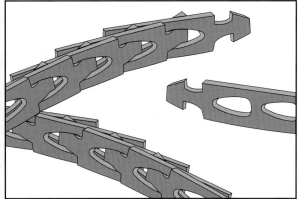

V-Belts You can find V-belts of various sizes at any automotive store (or you may have to special-order one from the manufacturer). Take your old belt with you to make sure you get the right size replacement.

Link Belts Although more expensive than standard V-belts, interlocking belts are sold by the foot and offer the advantage of custom sizing: By adding or subtracting links, you can make any diameter you want.

REPAIRING PORTABLE POWER PLANERS

For the most part, portable power planers are as rugged and dependable as other portable power tools. The big difference here, though, is that when the cutting knives of the tool become dull, there's more work involved to change them.

Unlike saw blades and drill bits, which can be changed in seconds, a power planer requires more time and attention—because cutterhead alignment is as critical here as it is with a jointer or planer.

With this in mind, it's well worth the time to check out how the knives are changed when you're looking to buy a new planer. Knife-changing routines run from amazingly simple to downright difficult.

If possible, ask a tool vendor to show you how the knives are changed. Also check the bed for flatness (*see Step 1 below*) before leaving the store. Reject any that aren't true and flat.

1 Check the bed Although most portable planers aren't used for precision work, it's still important that they make flat, true cuts. One thing to check for is to make sure the bed of the planer is flat. The simplest way to do this is to lay a known accurate straightedge along the length of the bed *as shown*. If you can see gaps between the bed and the straightedge, or if you find any gaps greater than 0.010" when using a feeler gauge, the bed needs to be flattened; proceed to Step 2. Otherwise, it's fine.

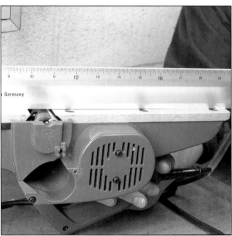

2 Flatten the bed To flatten the metal bed of a portable power planer, start by fully retracting the cutterhead. Most planers have a "park" position that sets the knives safely above the bed. Next, attach a couple sheets of silicon-carbide sandpaper to a known flat surface (such as a sheet of ¼"-thick tempered glass). Slide the plane over the sandpaper a few times, and examine the bed. Low spots will be shiny. Continue sanding the bed until it's flat.

3 Loosen knives As with any planer, the knives on a portable power planer will eventually dull and need to be sharpened or replaced. Knife changing varies from planer to planer. On some it's a pain; on others, like the Makita planer *shown here,* it's a breeze. Consult your owner's manual for specific directions. Quality planers will include a wrench for loosening the knife-mounting bolts. Following the manufacturer's directions, loosen the appropriate bolts and remove those as directed.

4 Remove/replace knives Most knives are held in place with brackets. After you've removed the bolts, lift off the bracket and slide out the planer knife (*see the photo at left*). The Makita planer *shown here* uses a unique blade retainer that virtually guarantees proper placement when the knives are re-installed. The edge of the retainer that's opposite the cutting edge has a lip that fits in a groove in the cutterhead; as long as the blade is aligned on the retainer (*see Step 3*), repositioning the knife is amazingly easy.

5 Adjust Depending on the manufacturer of your planer, it may or may not come with some sort of blade-alignment gauge. The planer *shown here* comes with a simple gauge that automatically aligns the planer knife in its retainer. Just position the knife with the retainer on the gauge, push the knife forward so that it contacts the lip of the gauge, and tighten the retainer screws (*see the photo at left*). It's that simple.

TROUBLESHOOTING

The jointer and the planer are two of the workshop's most reliable performers—as long as they are maintained regularly and kept in good condition. But being reliable also has its drawbacks. Depending on use, it can be a long time before the blades need to be removed and resharpened.

Because these tasks are required so infrequently, many woodworkers tend to shy away from correcting problems with their jointer or planer. It's not that it's so difficult to remedy the problem; it's just that it's an unfamiliar procedure—there's no confidence built up from repeatedly doing it.

I've seen the same thing with band saws—woodworkers continuing to use a dull blade because they're not comfortable with blade removal, installation, and adjustment.

If this is how you feel about your jointer or planer, I suggest that you take a rainy afternoon to build the necessary confidence.

Take the knives out of the jointer or planer, re-install and adjust them, and then do it again. Repeat as necessary until you're comfortable with the procedure. You'll be glad you did when you do encounter a problem with one of these machines.

In this chapter, I'll go over the most common problems you're likely to encounter with a jointer or a planer. I'll start by looking at what to do when your jointer is leaving a rough cut (*opposite page*) or is chipping out (*page 114*). Then on to what to do when the jointer isn't making straight, flat cuts (*page 115*) or is leaving a ribbed cut (*page 116*).

Next, there's information on how to correct a jointer that produces a rippled or burned cut (*page 117*), the motor bogs down (*page 118*), or it "snipes" the end of a workpiece as the trailing end passes over the cutterhead (*page 119*). And finally, what to do about excess vibration on a jointer (*page 120*).

The rest of the chapter is devoted to the planer, starting with the common causes of the all too familiar "snipe" (a dished cut at the beginning or end of a workpiece) and some solutions (*page 121*). Next, there are recommended fixes for a ribbed cut (*page 122*), a rough cut (*page 123*), and chip-out (*page 124*).

Finally, there's information on what causes a planer's motor to bog down and what you can do to prevent it (*page 125*).

Problem One of the most common complaints regarding a jointer's performance is that it produces a rough cut (*see the photo at left*). Instead of being smooth, the surface of the wood may have patches of lifted grain, there may be areas of chip-out or tear-out, or the entire surface may be rough. Although this is occasionally caused by the wood—in particular, woods with highly figured or squirrelly grain (such as burls, crotches, or bird's-eye)—it's more often caused by dull knives and by feeding the wood in the wrong direction (*see below*).

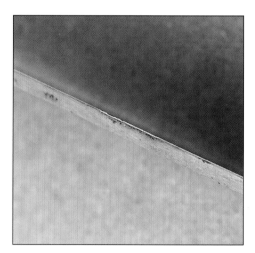

Dull Knives The leading cause of rough or poor cuts on a jointer is dull knives. How can you tell whether your knives are dull? If you shine a light directly on the edge of a knife and you see any reflection—like the reflection on the edge of the knife *shown here*—it's dull. In some cases, a quick stroke or two with a honing jig (*see page 94*) or oilstone can bring back the edge. Otherwise, you'll need to remove the knives and sharpen them yourself (*see pages 95–96*) or send them out for sharpening.

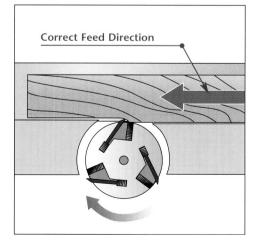

Correct Feed Direction

Wrong Direction The other common cause of a rough cut on a jointer is feeding the wood into the cutterhead with the grain going in the wrong direction. For the smoothest possible cut, the grain should slope down and away from the cutterhead, *as shown in the drawing at left.*

In a perfect world, this is always possible. But any woodworker knows that grain can switch direction in a piece of wood—often multiple times. In cases like this, try to joint the piece so that the majority of the grain is sloping down and away—and take a very light cut.

Jointers and Planers

Problem Chip-out on the jointer, particularly when you're jointing the edge, is another common problem (*see the photo at right*). Chip-out occurs when the knives pull up or tear out small pieces or chips of wood instead of severing the wood fibers. Here again, this can be caused by dull blades or by feeding the wood in the wrong direction (*see page 113*). It can also result from feeding the workpiece too fast or using a jointer with a chipped bed; *see below.*

Feed Rate Too Fast Assuming that your knives are sharp and that you're feeding the wood in the right direction, chip-out can and will occur if your feed rate is too fast. If you think about it, the faster the wood moves past the cutterhead, the harder the knives have to work to remove the same amount of wood. It's analogous to trying to pare off ½" of wood with a chisel in a single stroke—odds are that the wood will split or tear out. Slowing down the feed rate allows the knives to take more cuts, resulting in less of a chance of chip-out.

Chipped Bed Another reason wood can chip or tear out when jointing is that the wood fibers may not be supported during the cut. Just as the chip breaker on a hand plane helps to prevent chip-out by breaking off wood chips and fibers lifted by the blade, the edges of the jointer table near the cutterhead do the same thing. If the bed of your jointer is chipped (*as shown in the drawing at right*), it can't support the workpiece and help sever long chips and fibers.

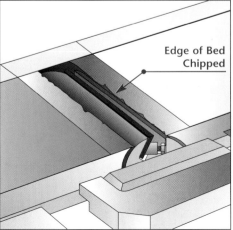

Edge of Bed Chipped

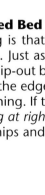

Problem A jointer that doesn't make flat cuts isn't worth beans. If a freshly jointed workpiece doesn't have perfectly perpendicular sides but instead makes a tapered or angled cut, like the one *shown in the photo at left,* you've got a real problem. Assuming that your fence is perpendicular to the table, a tapered cut like this is most likely caused by a warped bed or misaligned knives. If you've just adjusted your knives, odds are that one or more of them is out of alignment (*see below*).

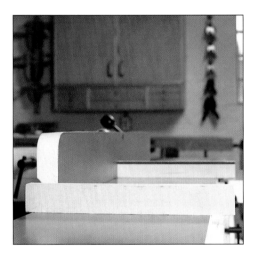

Warped Bed To check to see whether a tapered cut is being caused by a warped table, make a pair of "winding sticks" (*see the photo at left*). Place the sticks on the tables a couple inches in from each edge. Then sight along the sticks at a low angle to check for twist. If you detect a twist, there are some things to check for (*see pages 86–87*). If fixing those things doesn't cure the twist, the table will need to be reground.

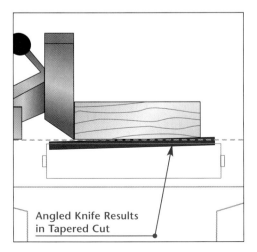

Angled Knife Results
in Tapered Cut

Knives Out of Alignment Hopefully, your table isn't warped, and your tapered cut is most likely caused by misaligned knives. If one or more of the knives is not parallel to the table, it'll produce a tapered cut (*see the drawing at left*). The solution is to check all your knives with the stick method (*see pages 89–90*) or a dial indicator (*see page 91*) to find the offending knife and align it with the rest of the knives.

Jointers and Planers

JOINTER:
RIBBED CUT

Problem Any woodworker who has inadvertently hit an embedded staple, nail, screw, or other piece of metal will recognize the photo *at right.* The convex-shaped rib near the bottom of the photo that runs the length of the workpiece was caused by nicked knives. Even the most careful woodworkers experience this every now and then. We grimace, shake our head, and stop the jointer to inspect the damage. There are two remedies to this problem: one long-term, and one short-term; *see below.*

Regrinding Nicked Knives The long-term solution to dealing with nicked knives is to remove them, have them reground, and then re-install them. Note that I don't suggest trying to regrind the knives yourself – a nick like the one *shown in the photo at right* would require hours and hours of work on a sharpening stone. Unless you have a system like the Tormek (*described on page 31*), it's best to drop your knives off at a professional sharpening service for regrinding.

Shifting a Nicked Knife Nicked knives don't have to shut you down. Instead, you can work around the problem with this temporary fix. Loosen one of the gibs so that it's friction-tight, and shift the knife to the left or right just far enough to offset the nick. Check the knife height and then retighten.

Since the shifted knife will be doing the work of three in the area of the nick, it will dull more quickly and can result in a rough cut. That's why this is just a temporary fix—as soon as possible, you should have the knife or knives reground.

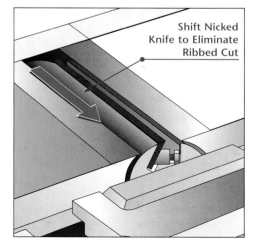

Shift Nicked Knife to Eliminate Ribbed Cut

Rippled Cut A rippled cut, where you can see tiny ridges on the edge of the board (*like those shown in the photo at left*) is yet another problem that can be encountered on the jointer. If you were to magnify these tiny ridges, you'd see that they are concave-shaped to match the arc of the cutterhead. They're basically the scooped cut that a knife makes as the wood is passed over the cutterhead.

Burn Marks If you hesitate in the middle of a cut on the jointer, you'll end up with a burn mark or scorch mark like the one *shown in the photo at left.* This is especially noticeable on lighter woods, and particularly cherry, which has the well-deserved reputation for burning if you look at it sideways.

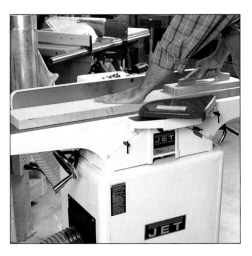

Adjusting the Feed Rate The solution to both of the problems above is to adjust the feed rate. In the case of the rippled cut, you're moving the workpiece over the cutterhead too fast. Slowing down the feed rate will allow the knives to make more cuts—in effect, you'll have a closer-spaced arc that won't be noticeable. If burning occurs, your feed rate is too slow. Keep the workpiece moving at a steady pace, and don't hesitate or stop during the cut.

Jointers and Planers

JOINTER:
MOTOR BOGS DOWN

Problem   You can tell when a jointer motor bogs down by its sound. Its normal whine will drop noticeably lower as it struggles to maintain a specified RPM. A couple of things happen when a motor bogs down, none of them good. Fewer RPM means slower knives, which results in a rougher cut.

A motor that's struggling is also going to run hotter, which will shorten its life. Bench-top jointers, with their small universal motors, are prone to this as they're often asked to do more than they can handle.

Feed Rate or Dull Knives   Assuming that your jointer is large enough to handle the task at hand, if your motor bogs down during the cut, it could be caused by too fast of a feed rate—you're asking it to remove wood more quickly than it can handle—or it could be that your knives are dull. When knives are dull, they don't cleanly shear the wood fibers; instead there's a lot of tearing, and so the motor has to work harder. As long as you use a moderate feed rate and sharp knives, this shouldn't be a problem.

Cutting Too Deep   Another reason a motor will bog down is that you're trying to take too deep of a cut in a single pass. This is particularly true with denser woods. Most jointer manufacturers list the recommended maximum cut in the owner's manual. Remember that the wider the workpiece, the lighter the cut should be, as you're removing a lot more wood. This is especially true when face-jointing: The lighter the cut, the better. Take your time—your patience will pay off.

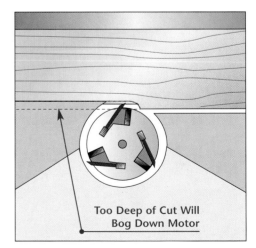

Too Deep of Cut Will
Bog Down Motor

Problem Although most woodworkers associate snipe (the dished-out cut at the end of a cut) with planers, it can also occur on a jointer (*see the photo at left*). Unlike with the planer, where snipe to some degree is always present, you can eliminate snipe entirely on the jointer with either a simple adjustment or with the proper technique; *see below.*

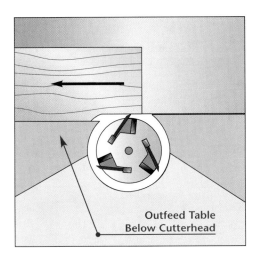

Outfeed Table
Below Cutterhead

Outfeed Table Misaligned Snipe can occur on the jointer if the outfeed table is adjusted below the cutterhead instead of being aligned with the top of its arc (*see the drawing at left*). When the outfeed table is below the cutterhead, the workpiece will "fall" into the knives as soon as the trailing edge is no longer supported by the infeed table. If your outfeed table is adjustable, raise it. Otherwise, you'll need to adjust the knives to match the height of the outfeed table (*see pages 88–93*).

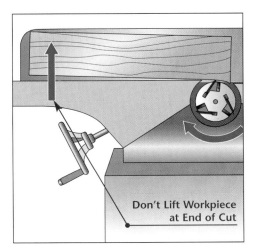

Don't Lift Workpiece
at End of Cut

Lifting Workpiece at End of Cut The other situation in which snipe can occur on a jointer is if the workpiece is lifted at the end of the cut (*see the drawing at left*). Lifting the leading edge of the workpiece will force the trailing end into the cutterhead, resulting in a dished cut. The solution is proper technique: Keep the workpiece level as you finish the cut, and transfer your weight to the outfeed table as the cut nears its end.

JOINTER:
EXCESS VIBRATION

Problem Besides rust, vibration is one of the biggest enemies of a power tool. Excess vibration can significantly shorten bearing life, can cause parts to rub together and wear quickly, and just as importantly, can create inaccurate cuts. I've always used the old nickel-on-its-edge trick to check vibration. With the tool running, you should be able to balance a nickel on its edge, *as shown in the photo at right.* If you can't, then it's time to take corrective action; *see below.*

Motor Loose If you are experiencing excess vibration of your jointer, start by checking to make sure that the motor is firmly attached to its mount. Then check with a level to ensure that the motor pulley and jointer pulley are aligned. If they're not, adjust one so that the pulleys are in the same plane. Check to make sure that the pulley setscrews are tight as well. A chipped or broken pulley will spin out of balance, which can also introduce vibration, as can a worn-out or kinked drive belt.

Stand Loose Once you're sure that the motor, its pulleys, and the drive belt are in good shape, you should check the stand. If the stand is metal (*like the one shown here*), work around the stand, checking each nut and bolt to make sure that they're tight. For wood stands, inspect the joints and repair any loose ones. Then check the tool-to-stand connection, and tighten as necessary.

Finally, most stands will benefit from added weight—you may be surprised to see how well a couple tubes or bags of sand will help dampen vibration.

Problem Snipe is so prevalent on most planers that many woodworkers think it's normal. It has become so accepted that many woodworkers routinely cut their boards an extra 6" to 8" long so that they can cut off the snipe on both ends. What a waste of time and good wood!

As with snipe on a jointer, snipe on the planer can be caused by an improperly adjusted machine, or by using incorrect technique—both of which can usually be remedied (*see below*).

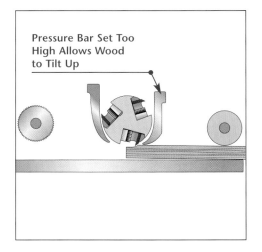

Pressure Bar Set Too
High Allows Wood
to Tilt Up

Feed Rollers Out of Adjustment Snipe on the planer is often caused by a pressure bar or outfeed roller that's set too high (*see the drawing at left*). In either case, the workpiece can tilt or spring up into the cutterhead once the trailing edge of the workpiece passes out from under the infeed roller. Check your owner's manual for the recommended adjustment procedure, and make the necessary adjustments.

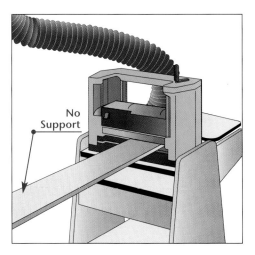

No
Support

No Support Another common cause of planer snipe is not supporting the workpiece throughout the entire cut. Basically, the workpiece tilts on the table edge and the end of the board lifts up into the cutterhead. Snipe can occur at the beginning of the cut as well as at the end if the board is not supported (*see the drawing at left*).

A good set of well-adjusted infeed and outfeed tables will go a long way toward preventing this from happening (*see page 11*). Roller supports (*see pages 28 and 80–83*) can also be used to support the workpiece to reduce the likelihood of snipe.

Jointers and Planers

PLANER:
RIBBED CUT

Problem Occasionally, you'll encounter a ribbed or rippled cut like the one *shown in the photo at right.* This problem shows itself as a set of regularly spaced indentations (or lines) across the face of the workpiece or as tiny scalloped ridges. The key to both is that the ridges or lines are equally spaced. In one case, the problem is caused by the feed rollers; the other is caused by feed rate (*see below*).

Feed Roller Pressure Excessive Equally spaced indentations like the ones *shown in the photo above* are caused by the serrated edges of a metal outfeed roller. This occurs when either the roller is too close to the workpiece or the spring pressure is excessive. In either case, the solution is to check your owner's manual for the recommended procedure and make any necessary adjustments (*see the photo at right*).

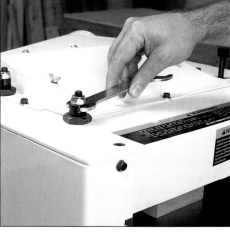

Feed Rate Too Fast Rippled cuts on the planer are often caused by using too fast a feed rate. For planers with multiple speeds, select a slower feed rate. Ripple cuts shouldn't occur on a single-speed planer unless you try to alter the feed rate by pushing or pulling the workpiece through the machine (*see the photo at right*). This generally isn't a good idea, as the feed rollers are designed to move the workpiece at the optimal speed. If a workpiece stalls or stops, adjust the cutterhead for a lighter cut instead of pulling or pushing the workpiece.

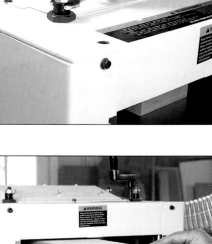

Problem A common complaint about a planer is that it produces a rough cut, like the one *shown in the photo at left.* The surface of the wood may be dimpled (the slight depressions seen on the wood *in the photo*), or there may be patches of lifted grain or chip-out.

As with the jointer, this may be caused by the wood—in particular, woods with highly figured or squirrelly grain (such as burls, crotches, and bird's-eye)—but it's more often caused by dull knives; dimples are caused by improper dust collection (*see below*).

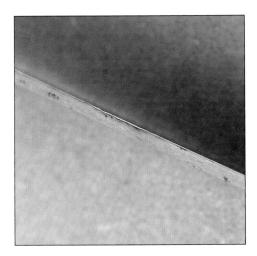

Dull Knives Dull planer knives don't shear the wood cleanly. Instead they pull and tear the wood fibers. Just as with the jointer, you can tell whether your knives are dull by shining a bright light on their edges. If you can see a reflection, as you can on the knife *in the photo at left,* the knives need to be sharpened.

No Dust Collection The dimples shown on the surface of the wood *shown in the top photo above* are caused by improper dust collection. When the dust port of a planer clogs up (*like the one shown in the photo at left*), the chips have nowhere to go but back into the planer, where they're blown out onto the workpiece and bed. As the chip-covered workpiece passes under the outfeed roller, it presses the chips into the surface, creating depressions. Keeping the dust port clear and the dust collector turned on will remedy this.

PLANER:
CHIP-OUT

Problem Sometimes, even when your knives are sharp, your dust-collection system is working, and the wood isn't highly figured, you can still experience chip-out like that *shown in the photo at right.* When this occurs, there are a couple more things to check: You may be feeding the wood into the planer incorrectly, or the pressure bar may be out of adjustment (*see below*).

Wrong Direction If you feed wood into a planer so that the grain is slanting up toward the cutterhead (*as shown in the drawing at right*), the knives will tear out the unsupported wood fibers on the surface. When you feed wood into the planer, the grain of the wood should always slant down away from the cutterhead (*as shown in the drawing below*). Since grain often changes direction within a piece of wood, feed the wood in so that the majority of the grain slants down, and take lighter cuts.

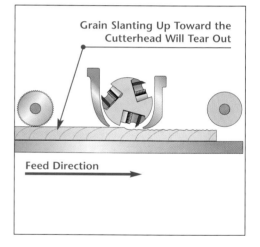

Grain Slanting Up Toward the Cutterhead Will Tear Out

Feed Direction

Chip Breaker Out of Adjustment If you're planer has an adjustable chip breaker and you're experiencing chip-out, it may be that your chip breaker is set too high (*see the drawing at right*). If it's not down pressing against the workpiece, it can't support the fibers being cut in front of it, and chip-out will occur. Consult your owner's manual for the recommended procedure, and make any necessary adjustments.

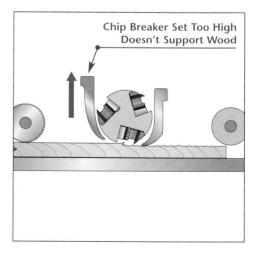

Chip Breaker Set Too High Doesn't Support Wood

Problem   As with a jointer, the sound that a planer's motor makes will let you know if it's working too hard. Here again, a drop in tone means that the motor is laboring to keep up its rated RPM. This results in slower knives and a rougher cut; running a motor too hot will also significantly reduce its lifespan. When the motor bogs down, it's telling you that you're trying to take too much off in a single pass or that your knives are dull (*see below*).

Cut Too Deep   If you try to remove too much wood in a single pass, the motor won't be able to handle it. This is particularly so when planing wide boards. The wider the board, the more wood the planer is removing, and the lighter the cut you should take. When you do take too deep a cut and the planer bogs down, the workpiece will often pause or hesitate. This can result in the surface being burned or burnished and will leave marks across the width of the workpiece (*see the photo at left*).

Dull Knives   Dull knives are another reason the motor on a planer will bog down. Instead of cleanly shearing wood fibers, the knives will pull and tear the wood. The harder the knives have to work, the more the motor will bog down. As always, this is most noticeable when planing wide stock. Hone the knives in place (*see page 94*), or remove them for sharpening (*see the photo at left*).

Jointers and Planers

GLOSSARY

Bed roller – an optional roller in the bed of many large stationary planers; the rollers are installed slightly above the bed to help reduce friction when feeding stock through the planer.

Bench-top jointer – a jointer that is designed for small spaces; it has a short bed and typically has an adjustable-speed universal motor.

Bench-top planer – a portable planer with a universal motor that can handle stock up to around 13" in width; both infeed and outfeed rollers are rubber, so the machine doesn't handle rough stock as well as a stationary planer does.

Bevel-cut – jointing at an angle from face to face of a workpiece, through its thickness and along its length.

Brush – a carbon composite shaped like a bar that maintains contact with the revolving armature in a universal motor, typically spring-loaded.

Carbide knives – knives made of solid carbide designed for heavy-duty use; although they require less-frequent sharpenings, they are much more brittle than high-speed steel knives and so nick easily.

Carbide-tipped knives – a hybrid of solid carbide and high-speed steel (HSS) knives; a strip of carbide is joined to the edge of a HSS knife to create a knife that lasts longer than HSS but is less expensive than solid carbide.

Chamfer – a decorative bevel jointed along the edge of a workpiece—typically at 45 degrees.

Chip breaker – a metal bar found in larger stationary jointers in front of the cutterhead; it presses against the workpiece and helps break off wood fibers before they can chip or tear out.

Cup – a form of warp that is an edge-to-edge curve across the face of a board; easily removed by face-jointing on the jointer.

Cut capacity – the manufacturer's recommended maximum depth of cut of a planer or a jointer; also the maximum width or thickness of a piece of wood that a planer can handle.

Cutterhead – a revolving spindle that holds the cutting knives of a planer or jointer; the knives fit in slots and are held in place with gibs.

Dial caliper – an accurate measuring device used to measure the thickness of a workpiece; the workpiece is inserted between the tips of the caliper, and the thickness is read on a dial calibrated in sixty-fourths of an inch.

Dial indicator – a measuring device that when fitted with a magnetic base can be used to accurately adjust the height of jointer knives.

Dust port – a metal, plastic, or wood hood that covers the dust chute of a planer or jointer to funnel chips and dust into the dust-collection system via a flexible hose.

Edge-jointing – using a jointer to plane off thin shavings of wood along the edge of a workpiece to make it true and flat.

Face-jointing – using a jointer to plane off thin shavings from the face of a workpiece to make it true and flat.

Feed rate – the rate at which a workpiece is fed into the cutterhead of a planer or jointer; this rate often affects the quality of cut.

Fence – an adjustable metal guide that runs perpendicular to the cutterhead; it can be angled to allow for bevel cuts.

Gib – a plate of metal machined to hold other parts in place, to afford a bearing surface, or to provide means for taking up wear.

Guard – a spring-loaded safety device designed to cover the exposed cutterhead of a jointer; it pivots out of the way to allow a workpiece to pass over the cutterhead without exposing the knives.

High-speed steel (HSS) – a steel alloy used to produce jointer and planer knives because of its durability when exposed to heat and vibration.

Hone – to finely sharpen the edge of a knife, typically with a small oilstone or whetstone.

Induction motor – a type of motor, found on larger stationary planers and jointers, that doesn't use brushes and that is capable of delivering much greater horsepower than universal motors.

Infeed – the part of a machine's table that is in front of the cutterhead.

Infeed roller – a roller on the infeed side of a planer's cutterhead that pulls and pushes the workpiece into the cutterhead; portable planers typically have rubber rollers, while stationary planers usually have serrated metal rollers to afford a better grip on rough-sawn stock.

Kickback – the tendency of a workpiece to be thrown back in the direction of the operator of the machine.

Magnetic knife-setting jig – a jig that incorporates a series of strong magnets to hold jointer or planer knives in position while the gibs are tightened; one set of magnets holds the knives, and the other set grips the cutterhead.

Molding cutters – a set of metal knives, shaped in a variety of profiles, used in planer/molders to make molding.

Multipurpose machine – any machine that provides multiple functions, such as a planer/molder or a jointer/planer; both parts of the machine share a single cutterhead.

Outfeed – the part of a machine's table that is behind the cutterhead.

Outfeed roller – a roller on the outfeed side of the cutterhead that pulls and pushes the workpiece past the cutterhead and out of the machine; usually made

of rubber so as not to damage the freshly planed surface.

Pawls – small, pivoting metal levers with sharp ends that are designed to grip the workpiece and prevent it from being kicked back toward the operator.

Portable power planer – a small hand-held power tool that is effectively an electric hand plane; they're capable of removing up to $\frac{1}{16}$" of material in a single pass.

Pressure bar – a metal bar on the outfeed side of the cutterhead on a stationary planer that presses the workpiece firmly into the bed of the planer.

Push block – a safety device used on the jointer to feed a workpiece over the cutterhead, thereby protecting the operator's hands.

Rabbet – a step-like cut in the edge or end of a workpiece, usually made to form part of a joint.

Raised panel – a panel with beveled edges that fit into grooves cut in the rails and stiles of a frame.

Roller support – an auxiliary stand positioned on either the infeed or outfeed side of a jointer or planer to support the workpiece; the workpiece rides on one or more rollers to reduce friction.

Snipe – a dished cut, typically at the end of a planer's cut, caused by inadequate support or by an improperly adjusted planer.

Stationary jointer – any jointer with a 6" or wider cutterhead that has long tables and an induction motor.

Stationary planer – any planer with a cutterhead wider than 13" that uses an induction motor.

Stick method – a low-tech method that uses a stick to adjust the height of the knives of a jointer.

Taper – an angled cut along the length of a workpiece that reduces the width of the workpiece at one end.

Tear-out – the tendency of a cutterhead to tear the fibers of the workpiece, leaving a ragged surface instead of cutting them; typically caused by a dull blade.

Thickness-plane – to reduce the thickness of a workpiece so that the two faces end up parallel.

Universal motor – a small motor that uses brushes to maintain contact between the wiring and the rotating armature; typically capable of delivering only low horsepower.

V-belt – a continuous rubber belt that connects the motor of a stationary power tool to the cutterhead or drive system; the bottom of the belt is V-shaped to fit into the V-shaped grooves in the pulleys.

Way – the guiding surface on the bed of a machine, along which a table or carriage moves.

Winding sticks – narrow strips of wood placed on the tables of a jointer to check for twist.

INDEX